Everybody has junk they need to deal with, or at least they ought to deal with. In *Throw It Down*, Jud challenges us to face our junk and deal with it so we can become all God desires us to be. Filled with great insights and raw stories of recovery and hope, this is a fantastic resource for anyone wanting to grow.

MARK BATTERSON, lead pastor of
National Community Church;
author of *In a Pit with a Lion on a Snowy Day* and *Primal*

I want to stick this book in the hands of each and every person who is struggling with some kind of addiction in their life. I'm not sure if I've ever seen the process of "freedom" so clearly articulated by anyone! Clearly, Jud Wilhite is passionate about people discovering freedom from the things that are holding them back from who God wants them to become.

PETE WILSON, lead pastor of Crosspoint.tv;
author of *Plan B*

Jud Wilhite and his team have been instrumental in helping thousands discover freedom. Now he brings these stories and learnings into a powerful look at how God can set each of us free. Real-life change is possible, and Jud shows the way clearly and convincingly.

CRAIG GROESCHEL, founding pastor of LifeChurch.tv;
author of *The Christian Atheist*

I am someone who has dealt with addictive and self-destructive behaviors much of my adult life, and who is also trying to pursue a healthy relationship with God and with others. Jud's book truly hits the mark. It's informative, heartfelt, biblical; and it weaves in the stories of other people suffering from a variety of addictions and types of brokenness while keeping redemption in the center. *Throw It Down* is beautifully written, and each page is full of grace and healing.

ANNE JACKSON, speaker; author of
Permission to Speak Freely; blogger at FlowerDust.net

THROW IT DOWN

Leaving Behind Behaviors and Dependencies that Hold You Back

JUD WILHITE

ZONDERVAN® A WORTHY BOOK

ZONDERVAN.com/
AUTHORTRACKER
follow your favorite authors

ZONDERVAN

Throw It Down
Copyright © 2010 by Jud Wilhite

This title is also available as a Zondervan ebook. Visit www.zondervan.com/ebooks.

This title is also available in a Zondervan audio edition. Visit www.zondervan.fm.

Requests for information should be addressed to:

Zondervan, *Grand Rapids, Michigan 49530*

Library of Congress Cataloging-in-Publication Data

Wilhite, Jud.
   Throw it down : leaving behind behaviors & dependencies that hold you back /
 by Jud Wilhite.
      p. cm.
   ISBN 978-0-310-32753-0 (hardcover, jacketed)
   1. Success—Religious aspects—Christianity.   2. Habit breaking—Religious
aspects—Christianity. 3. Dependency (Psychology) 4. Addicts—Religious life.
I. Title. II. Title: Leaving behind behaviors & dependencies that hold you back.
III. Title: Leaving behind behaviors and dependencies that hold you back.
BV4598.3.W53 2010
248.8'629—dc22   2010034660

All Scripture quotations, unless otherwise indicated, are taken from the Holy Bible, *New Inter-national Version*®, *NIV*®. Copyright © 1973, 1978, 1984 by Biblica, Inc.™ Used by permission of Zondervan. All rights reserved worldwide. Scripture quotations marked NLT are taken from the *Holy Bible, New Living Translation,* copyright © 1996, 2004. Used by permission of Tyndale House Publishers, Inc., Wheaton, Illinois. All rights reserved. Scripture quotations marked MSG are taken from *The Message.* Copyright © 1993, 1994, 1995, 1996, 2000, 2001, 2002. Used by permission of NavPress Publishing Group. Scripture quotations marked NKJV are taken from the New King James Version. Copyright © 1982 by Thomas Nelson, Inc. Used by permission. All rights reserved.

Any Internet addresses (websites, blogs, etc.) and telephone numbers printed in this book are offered as a resource. They are not intended in any way to be or imply an endorsement by Zondervan, nor does Zondervan vouch for the content of these sites and numbers for the life of the book.

Published in association with Yates & Yates, www.yates2.com

Packaged by Worthy Media. For subsidiary and foreign language rights, contact info@worthy media.com

Cover design: Chris Tobias, Tobias Design
Cover photography: Corbis Images
Interior design: Inside Out Design and Typesetting

Printed in the United States of America

10 11 12 13 14 15 /DCI/ 25 24 23 22 21 20 19 18 17 16 15 14 13 12 11 10 9 8 7 6 5 4 3 2 1

To the recovery team at Central Christian Church who give so much to help others experience freedom.

Contents

1
The Road Out

I *wake sometime deep in the night, heart pounding frenetically on a cocktail of drugs, shivering in a cold sweat, my own saliva spilled in thick threads onto my face and chest. Barely able to rise and stand, I look in the mirror and the morose images swim around my head: purple sores, hollow cheeks, lost weight, vacant eyes. Seventeen and going on ninety, I no longer care about the terrible risk of recapturing a high that increasingly eludes me.*

Gathering myself, I line up my considerable stash and take it all. I surrender myself to the mercy of the drugs. For the longest time, coming in and out of consciousness, I find myself gripping the bumper of my old red Fiero, throwing up violently, finding a strange comfort in the fact I will soon be dead . . .

Later, I come to. Every part of my body hurts. As I wake, I feel the weight of a dark despair unhinging. The window blinds are pulled; I don't know what time of day (or even what day) it is. Lying on the floor too exhausted to move, I take in the soft and subdued light spilling around me. I am reminded somehow of grace. For the first time in my life, in the middle of my bottom, I desire to be free.

This book is about this desire for freedom and how I, along with many others, have experienced rescue, redemption, and hope. It *is* possible for you to be free and embrace the life God has for you. It *is* possible to become the person you were meant to be, the person you long to be. It *is* possible to experience life change.

We all have something we'd like to be freed from, something that holds us back. Maybe your issue is subtler than mine. Maybe you struggle with perfectionism. Perhaps you are addicted to approval. Anger could be wreaking havoc in your life. A manipulative approach toward people may be ruining every romantic relationship you've had. Maybe you overwork, overeat, overdrink, or overshop and eventually discover that you are being held captive. The very thing you desire, what you hope will set you free—enslaves you.

HOMECOMING

In the days following my nearly fatal overdose, I realize my lack of serious options. Exhausted by endless cycles of disappointment, hurt, suffering, and guilt, I come to understand at a very deep level my inability to save myself.

I can die, go crazy, or get help.

So I cry out. A few weeks after my overdose, I drop to my knees in my bedroom and say the only prayer I can muster: "God, help me. I'm messed up beyond belief. I need you." As my words dissipate, I listen to the sound of the unbalanced ceiling fan squeaking above me. No voice speaks audibly to me. In my heart, though, two words slowly take shape in my consciousness: Welcome home.

Only when I admitted my powerlessness to God did things begin to change. The Bible says, "The fear of the LORD is the beginning of wisdom, and knowledge of the Holy One is understanding" (Prov. 9:10). That fear doesn't mean we walk around in terror. It means that we revere and respect God. The foundational aspect of wisdom does not begin with a degree, but in a faith birthed in the character and nature of God.

A harmful habit is rarely the result of a thing we do, but an idol we create. In the false hope of satisfying our deepest cravings for significance, comfort, security, meaning, approval, and ultimately love, we often place our trust in alternative saviors and swear allegiances to artificial gods. We seek to design our own agendas rather than trust in a God who asks that we give away our lives for the sake of others.

When we place our faith in such tiny gods, we sin, which literally means to miss God's mark for our lives. We intrinsically and inevitably follow a path to heartache. Think of all the broken relationships and torn lives in the wake of greed, lust, gossip, and relentless pursuit of success. Consider, too, all the years of life wasted in self-destructive patterns and self-defeating behaviors.

WASTELAND EXODUS

In the midst of my four-year wasteland of addiction, my parents make me go to church. Promising to go to youth group, I walk through the church into nearby alleys, killing time by smoking cigarettes. I observe people walking into the church building, but I don't really understand the attraction. When I reconnect with my parents, we play out the same conversation.

"What did you learn about in church, son?"

"Jesus," I say.

"And what about Jesus?"

"That he loves me."

I answer in this way because I believe this is what they wish to hear.

Secretly, deep in my brokenness, it is what I long to believe.

The biblical book of Exodus, which literally means "the road out," provides deep insights about moving out of captivity. Exodus chronicles the journey of the Israelite people from slavery to a new life of freedom in ways deeply applicable to our own contemporary journeys.

From slavery, God led the people of Israel into freedom. In the ancient wisdom of the biblical narrative, the book of Exodus foreshadows the movement into the full life promised by Jesus. It begins and ends with God's redemption. Exodus explains the great lengths God went to in order to accomplish the liberation of his people. He reveals himself to be both *with* and *for* his people. By the power and grace of God, Exodus brings us back to our true selves, destinies, and stories. In the depth of a great desperation we are not only reminded but also empowered to take the road out. And like all great Old Testament stories, Exodus points to the reality of Jesus, who came to "heal the brokenhearted, to proclaim liberty to the captives" (Luke 4:18 NKJV). With a self-sacrificing love, Jesus bore the divine punishment and curse of sin, setting us free by God's power and grace.

All roads out eventually lead us to the love of Jesus.

My own road out of a deadly addiction eventually came full circle, leading me back to the church. Only God in his mercy and irony could take a messed-up kid lost in addiction, piece him back together, get him through college and graduate school, and deploy him in a place self-proclaimed the City of Sin. In Las Vegas, there are no culture wars. Morality lost. Built on a billion-dollar marketing machine, the city annually yields some of the highest rates in the nation for everything bad: drug use, domestic violence, addictions, and divorce.

Twenty-two years into my recovery, I pastor Central Christian Church, a church with campuses in unlikely places in Las Vegas and beyond. When tempted to despair against the long odds of ministry, I trace deep etchings of faith back to a day on the freeway, a few weeks after my nearly fatal overdose at the age of seventeen. Driving my red Fiero down a Texas interstate at seventy miles per hour, I found a supernatural power to throw my drugs out the window. In the days that follow, sweaty and clammy and grumpy, I understood the life-and-death nature of my circumstances and whispered my prayers continually: "I can't do this alone. God, help me. If you don't show up somewhere in my life, I'm through."

God gave me the grace to return to church on my own terms. Surrounded by a handful of people, I experienced recovery in a community of people who walked with me and listened and coached me off the edge. They were not scared away by my problems or doubts. God used the church to save my life. And then, through the church, the road led me back into the pain of a broken world.

I have seen Jesus' work in my own life, and in thousands in our church who experience freedom. Drugs should have killed me, and they almost did, but God provided the road out. A deep community of faith continues to sustain me in my life. Together, we have come to understand the irony of a power springing from powerlessness, and an overwhelming dependence on God that sets others and ourselves free. God's grace moves in power and love, often incognito, for the redemption of people trapped in the bondage of sin.

Together, we fight for freedom in the moment-by-moment reality of gratitude. We share what we experience through the person and work of Jesus, who lived, died, and rose again for our freedom. His sacrifice on the cross provided that path to pardon, and his resurrection opened up a road of life. Without shame, we follow him to find our true purpose—bringing glory to God, serving him, delighting in his freedom, and helping others walk in it.

No matter what you have done or where you have been, God in his love has made a road out from slavery to sin and self-defeating behaviors, a road to freedom. In the following pages, I'll share core principles that have freed thousands of people. I'll share the stories of several to inspire your own journey. Life change happens. Your future can look different. Tomorrow does not have to repeat the mistakes of yesterday.

For years, across the street from our original church campus in the Las Vegas area, strobe lights would shoot into the night sky from an adult bookstore. Directions to the church were easy: follow the lights to the "Live Nude Adult Bookstore" and turn right to the church. I like that because it's such a stark picture of repentance. We are all only a turn away from freedom.

So what's holding you down? What's weighing on you? You can break free. I know this can be scary, but see it as an opportunity. This is a chance to be free. Today, list the top three things holding you back from freedom with God, yourself, and others.

2
BEAUTIFUL SHAMBLES

If we are honest with ourselves, we know some of what holds our lives at bay — the particular destructive patterns, emotions, identities, or histories. And, if we have wrestled long enough, most of us would also admit to a growing powerlessness to do anything about it. That's a good thing — if we move past defeat to look up and depend on God for help.

While contemplating his plan for recovery, the same images play through Lance's head.[1] In his mind's eye, he first sees himself playing golf with his father, like he has twice a week for eighteen years, and then he startles with the phone's ring, bristling with the news of his dad's heart attack. Then he finds himself with his wife, on the morning of their ninth anniversary, gathered around the television, watching the slow and surreal implosion of the World Trade Center Towers from the force of two Boeing 767s—one of which he recognizes as a plane he had previously piloted.

Then his mind shifts to eighteen months later when, spirit deflated, he hands in his wings after an aviation career spanning thirty-five years.

Lance shakes his head to clear the images. He reminds himself of all the reasons they called him Captain—the discipline inherited from his military father, the perseverance from his polio-stricken mother, and the skill he used to rise to such heights of respect as a pilot. At fifty-eight, Lance believes the newly discovered holes in his life can be fixed. He must simply form the right plan.

Faced with the loss of his identity and a hint of mortality, he quickly comes to the conclusion that he feels no overwhelming need for God simply because he continues to invest in the concept of control. Plus, he harbors anger with God over his father's death and his mother's wheelchair. So, God? No. Close friends? No, he never really allowed for any. Family? No, they didn't really share those kinds of feelings.

And so, this is what Lance's logic chooses: why not a drink? It worked to put him at ease in social situations, and who could argue with the occasional college kegger or the Friday Night Happy Hour in the Officer's Club Stag Bar? He reasons alcohol is capable of taking the razor's edge off of his life, so he can fully engage his own plan for redemption.

HELP WANTED

Our habits often start innocently enough. Maybe you love to shop or enjoy eating great food. These are gifts from God. But if you allow these desires to run out of control, driven by a need to feel security or worth or love, you head straight for trouble. Shopping is great until you have fifty thousand dollars (and counting) on your credit cards. Food is wonderful until the doctor recommends a diet, and yet your soul is so starved you give into a compulsion to eat more.

Most of the idols we crave are good things allowed to take control. Sleep, food, sex, pleasure, and work are all God-designed realities for the good but, forced to extremes, yield laziness, obesity, lust, excess, and imbalance. Although we may not immediately recognize the dysfunction driving the behavior, we take the first steps on the road out to freedom by naming destructive patterns and recognizing that we can't find healing alone. By doing so, we honestly face the problem.

Sometimes God allows you to be placed in a position where there is nowhere left to turn but to him. In the middle of a struggle, it's tough to admit you can't handle it by yourself and you need help moving forward. Yet one of the greatest and most liberating moments in life occurs when you stop, reach out to God, and say the words, "I can't do this on my own." *Then* you are in a position to receive God's care and give him the glory for his work. An early church leader named Augustine put it like this: "God gives where he finds empty hands."

In other words, when you need help, recognize your need. Then ask for it, without pretending you're in a position to help yourself. Perhaps God has allowed you to be in that position so you will turn to him and acknowledge your need.

In the grip of a consuming addiction, Lance invests the next few years of his life in deceit—attempting to fill a secret supply of alcohol. He hides bottles in every room of his house, the back of toilets, the trunk of his car, his golf bag, even in a gas grill. Lance retreats into isolation, passionately fueling the void, abandoning any pretense of a social life or meaningful relationships. The darkness of his depression seldom sees the light of day. And, free from the random drug testing, he continues to up the ante on his wager that alcohol will help.

In response to his wife's plea to get help, Lance calmly tells her he will after his first arrest and, on that same day, finds himself sitting in a less-than-five-star room at the El Segundo Jail for a DUI. In the middle of the night he awakes from a nightmare and reminds himself to pick up a fifth of Scotch from the liquor store upon his release.

The next day he suffers seizures in a hotel lobby and, if not for the persistence of a security officer, believes his dead body would have been found later in his room. Lance spends the next two weeks—including four days with ankles and wrists strapped to a bed—convulsing in an ICU unit, in and out of consciousness, suffering from a combination of withdrawal, pneumonia, liver abnormalities, severe depression, and water on the brain.

Finally, Lance hits bottom. He knows it is "change or die" time. He sees his carefully controlled world in shambles. For the first time he admits he is powerless and cries out to God for help.

THE CHARACTER OF GOD

There are a lot of images of God out there in our culture. There's God as Morgan Freeman in *Bruce Almighty.* Superb posture, great narrative voice, really stylish dresser. There's God as an animated Victorian-era cartoon in *Monty Python and the Holy Grail.* Scary voice, no-nonsense attitude, hinged jaw, big crown, and robe. There's God as Ralph Richardson in *Time Bandits.* Conservative business suit, a well-groomed grandfather running out of energy.

Your view of God affects virtually everything in your life. In the book of Exodus, the character of God unfolds as the story develops. In the opening chapters, Israel cries out and God responds with compassion. He pays attention to the pain of his people. Exodus tells us that "God heard their groaning and he *remembered* his covenant with Abraham, with Isaac and with Jacob. So God *looked on* the Israelites and *was concerned* about them" (Exod. 2:24–25, emphasis mine).

In response to the suffering of his people, God places the context of his future work of redemption in a relationship of love.

- *He hears.* Imagine that the God of the universe actually hears your cry for help! He is not deaf to your need. Your prayers can reach God, and he will listen.
- *He remembers.* God remembers his relationship with you. He remembers your history, good and bad, but ultimately your intended position in a world created for his glory. He remembers that by redeeming you he is bringing glory to himself and honoring his nature.
- *He looks on.* God is not watching from a distance. He's watching you up close and personally. He's intimately involved in the details of your life.
- *He is concerned.* The word translated "concern" is used in a variety of ways from simple perception to a more intimate and relational knowledge. The point here is that *God has a longstanding relationship with*

his people. From the depths of his relationship, God's mercy and his intention to save flow like a mighty river. God is not standing idly by; rather, he is about to move. He is concerned, and he will save.

For a man once known as Captain, Lance knows the process of surrender will be a continuing one. He enters into a rehab program with some positive results and focuses on putting his faith and trust in Jesus. He gets intentional about his spiritual journey and finds a community of faith to help him grow.

Lance knows the road out will be a long one, and it starts with admitting that he can't do it on his own. His life has grown totally unmanageable. He starts to meet weekly with a recovery group and daily asks God for help. He knows there is no way to freedom without the day-by-day help of God. He doesn't get paralyzed with thoughts of tomorrow or next year; he focuses on trusting God and living free today. Slowly, painfully, he takes the steps to freedom.

After a year of sobriety, Lance seeks to make a public statement of his faith in Jesus, who empowers and sustains his healing. Before his baptism, he looks out over the church and sees the people he loves surrounding him. It is his wife, once again, who stands beside him, also declaring her faith in Jesus. Together, they share the understanding of a supernatural and graceful God working in power and love for them. Lance reflects on his former life of isolation in the sea of smiling faces — new friends who help in his rescue and family members in restored relationship. Once hidden and alienated in self-deception and secrets, his greatest joy is to share this moment with others.

For a man once known as Captain, the reality of powerlessness will be a place Lance revisits again and again. In contrast to his old self-assurance, Lance understands the power in his life change flows through the ongoing realization of a complete dependence on God. As he comes to grips with a freedom orchestrated only by the power and grace of God, he feels freed from the need to control his own life and surrenders with increasing joy to serving others.

"The first step of recovery is surrender," Lance says, "and my entire life had been based on being in control. I may never fully understand the circumstances and events that led to my nearly killing myself with alcohol, but I do now understand that I had a disease for which there is no cure. It

may have been lying dormant in my body like a cancer for many years and when it appeared there was no way I could control it. It makes it easier to surrender when you have no real choices."

Today Lance and his delightful wife give most of their free time to helping others experience recovery through Central Christian Church. As I've come to know Lance, the reality that always strikes me first is his smile—not just from ear to ear but rising up from a soul once broken and restless now healed and at peace. Lance isn't perfect, but he knows the One who is—the One who continues to not only restore but magnify his life.

At the very points of your deepest powerlessness, God reveals his character, love, and power to transform you. Whatever you're up against in life, think about what it means that God "hears," "remembers," "looks on," and "is concerned." He not only cares about your next breath, he cares about your entire journey through life into eternity.

Admit that you can't fully let go on your own. Sure,

you may be incredibly talented, strong, dynamic, and successful, but if you want to be free—well, that is something else. Freedom begins when you reach out to God and admit you are powerless and need his help.

Like Israel in its slavery, cry out to God in prayer. Throughout the Bible, you see short 9-1-1 prayers for help. For example, Psalm 109:26: "Help me, oh help me, GOD, my God, save me through your wonderful love" (MSG). The next time you stand in line to buy a new thing with money you don't have or scan the freezer for another ice cream sandwich you shouldn't eat or consider gossiping about a cousin you don't like or contemplate a business deal that would compromise your character, whisper a short prayer: "Help me, oh help me, God, my God. Save me through your wonderful love."

And then walk—or better, run—away.

The Bible says, "Through Christ Jesus the law of the Spirit of life set me free from the law of sin and death" (Rom. 8:2). When we surrender to Jesus, God's Spirit comes to dwell inside of us. It is the spirit of life, the inward principle, that moves us. Now we have the power to yield to the law of the spirit of life rather than the law of sin and death. Ask God's Spirit to help you face the challenges in your life. Depend on him and trust him to pull you through. He can set you free from sin and death!

3
THROW IT DOWN

Admitting we need the help of a God who desires our freedom establishes the possibility of change. Surrendering to God empowers that possibility. But what does it mean to surrender to God? For years, I wrongly believed in a God who mostly desired my boredom. If I surrendered to God, I believed I would end up losing who I am. I could see myself in a shirt with a pocket protector and plaid pants like a junior accountant. What I didn't understand was that, because he created me, God knows what makes me tick. And that when I surrendered to God, he would take me places that would optimize the design he'd built into me. There was nothing cheesy or boring about it. It was fulfilling.

In the movie *Return of the King* from the Lord of the Rings trilogy, such a personal transformation is accomplished in the character of Aragorn, the king whose return has been foretold. Having spent several years dodging the reality that he is heir to the throne, he has roamed Middle Earth as Strider the ranger, a sort of cross between mercenary, bounty hunter, and border-patrol guard. When Elrond, the king of the elves, hands the restored Sword of the West to Aragorn, he tells him, "It is time to put away the ranger and become that which you were created to be." This is what happens in surrender—we begin to discover the person God created us to be and the person we desire to become.

What You Call Home

After throwing down a fifth of mescal tequila with her friend, Ashley resonates to the possibilities of Las Vegas waking at midnight. Swallowing the worm from the bottom of the bottle, Ashley, a graduate from the University of Washington with a degree in political science, understands the cost. Having lost fifteen jobs in the five years since graduation, she fuses to the city's high-wire pursuit of ecstasy and escape. She longs to find the road out of herself or, at the very least, the pain that increasingly defines her.

When she howls at the moon, her friend suggests another bar, which leads to another bar, which leads to a closing drink at Shifty's Lounge, a biker's club. The sunrise seems to punctuate another story in an intertwined history of weed, meth, small-time dealing, alcohol, Harleys, gambling, and eluding the law—the surrender to the rush and blur of the Las Vegas lifestyle.

On the way home, Ashley's girlfriend passes out behind the wheel of a Firebird moving at seventy miles per hour. Hitting the median, the car flips and Ashley, unbuckled inside, rolls twice end over end before her face spiders the windshield and several ribs crack along the dashboard. Finally, she is thrown out the passenger-side window.

Coming to consciousness on the side of the road, pooled in her own blood from gaping head-to-toe wounds, Ashley does not feel overwhelming pain or trauma. Instead, she surrenders to a mysteriously strong sense of having been thrown down gently by a band of angels.

Years earlier, at the age of sixteen, Ashley's life first spun out of control. She remembers hanging up the phone in her *family's suburban home in Thousand Oaks, California, a mostly blue-sky reality of life residing between Malibu and Hollywood. That day, as the knot in her stomach tightened, she wondered how she would explain to her mother the news from the naval officer—the report of her brother's psychotic break with reality. Ashley already felt as if it didn't matter if she went left or right; her mother could never be pleased. She couldn't help but think what new abuse this circumstance might ignite.*

But her greater fear populated the idea of losing her brother. In the general absence of their father, a prestigious pilot with women in other cities, and the emotional distance of their mother, the two of them counted on each other for survival. All the early family photos show them together, and even now she considers Sean her best friend. They formed a team against long odds.

When she told her mother a short time later that her son had been transferred to a mental ward for observation, Ashley's mother collapsed onto a kitchen bench, eyes glazing, a permanent vacancy settling.

Over the next years, a variety of diagnoses—manic-depressive, schizophrenic, schizo-effective—were shoveled on Sean as Ashley watched her brother slowly deteriorate into a shell of his vibrant and sweet-souled self. With each of Sean's stays in a series of institutions, psychiatric wards, jails, hospitals, halfway houses, VA facilities, and the streets, Ashley not only had to deal with the losses but also with the accusations of her mother, who increasingly blamed her for not providing the love, care, and support she deemed necessary.

Ashley has retreated into her newfound loves of alcohol, weed, and her boyfriend at the same time she exhausts herself trying, to the best of her intoxicated ability, to care for her brother and please a demanding mother who will never be pleased. She fears not so much falling into a cycle of abuse, but learning to call it home.

Following her near-fatal accident and years of addiction to numb her pain and feelings of failure, when a friend suggests that God was trying to get her attention, she senses an inconsistency between who she has become and who she was created to be. She begins to attend church, participate in rehab, and cut back on her party lifestyle.

More than eighteen months later, smoking a bowl of marijuana at her father's house, she realizes the distance *between her efforts to heal and the still-painful reality of her life. In a moment of heart-wrenching clarity, she rises to go to the bathroom and sees her reflection in the mirror: bloated red face, angry countenance, a total loser, a person headed nowhere. She's thirty and alone, living with her father, blowing up his chimney the smoke of weed that she purchased after pilfering his wallet.*

She packs another bowl, kneels again by the fireplace, and feels the familiar stab of pain in her knee, the most enduring reminder of her near-fatal accident. Rising with the smoke is Ashley's prayer of surrender. For the first time in her life, she understands how much the realization of her true self depends on the power and love of God.

Two days later, after another friend tells her she can't do it alone, Ashley returns to her father's home, drinks the remaining beer in his refrigerator, and makes an appointment to attend her first AA meeting.

EXCUSES, EXCUSES

When Moses first met God in a burning bush and he received the divine calling to lead Israel to freedom, he responded with logical doubts. Who was he—a Hebrew wandering as a shepherd in a wasteland of exile — to confront the most powerful person on the planet? And suppose that the pharaoh didn't know the name of Moses' God? And what if no one listened to his outrageous demand to set the Israelites free?

In his broken humanity, Moses stood in good company. Reluctance and failure to surrender immediately to God's plan marked the life of many of God's leaders in the Old Testament. Gideon felt insignificant. Samuel feared God's mission for his life would trouble a relationship with his friend and mentor. Isaiah believed he was too dirty and tainted. Jeremiah reasoned he was too young and uneducated. In the middle of each person's doubts, God accomplished his loving transformation. Gideon rose to become a mighty warrior; Samuel, Isaiah, and Jeremiah became some of the greatest of God's prophets.

Excuses stand in the way of God's design and purpose for your life. Do you hold onto bitterness against someone who has abused you or refuses to change? Do you turn to a destructive habit — maybe nonstop work or constant gossip — to help you feel better? Do you believe you can prevent an addiction from spinning out of control? Are you walking around in pain—from a divorce or a death—building strong walls to keep out more pain?

To lay down a crippling emotion or habit requires surrender. You must move from believing God to be out there somewhere to trusting him to know what heals you and lead you on the road to freedom. You must see your excuses for what they are: lame attempts to avoid the deeper issues blocking the potential healing God desires to accomplish.

What's in Your Hand?

Thirteen years into sobriety, Ashley receives word of a good friend, also years into recovery, who hangs herself in despair after falling back into addiction. She knows the power of the disease. From her own experience, she understands that even the force of being thrown out the passenger-side window of a speeding car is not necessarily enough to bring one to surrender.

At the same time, against long odds, she finds hope by learning to listen to the whispers of God. "I continually ask God what he wants me to do. And then I listen. That does not mean I always follow what he wants me to do. So surrendering occurs when I listen to his suggestions—because he is a gentleman and does not force me to do anything. But I've learned when I do it my way it usually hurts a lot worse. Sometimes I ask him in anger, 'What do you want from me?' and then he waits for me to calm down and whispers some more to me."

Through her experience and the community recovery programs in which she involves herself, she feels privileged to offer that same hope to others, even if it might be only a whisper: I know where you are at, and it is not beyond the rescuing love and power of God.

In the process of ongoing surrender, Ashley finds a new identity as a loved child of God. "My Higher Power is Jesus, and he is around 24/7 to help me anytime I need it. He is my reason for living, and after all these years we are still strong. He is my best friend. He never leaves me nor forsakes me. He is always with me."

In the presence of God, Moses quickly learned the value of surrender on the journey from captivity to freedom. Following a series of excuses from Moses, God decided to give him a visual lesson on the power of surrender. They engaged in the following conversation:

THE LORD: What's that in your hand?

MOSES: A staff.

THE LORD: Throw it on the ground.

I believe the staff represents the identity of Moses—his career as a shepherd and his living income. When God asked him to throw it down, an act of surrender was required from Moses. God was saying, "Release that thing you are holding onto that represents your core identity, income, career, and life. Throw it down before me."

When Moses did as he was asked, the staff became a snake and he ran away in fear. But God told him to pick it up again, and when he did, it once again became a piece of wood. The transformation mirrored the transformation Moses would go through—from shepherd to shepherd-leader. God turned that staff into a sign of Moses' new occupation. He was now the shepherd and leader of God's people. After Moses picked up the staff, it was called "God's rod" and Moses was "God's person." By the love and power of God, Moses would be suited for his new identity.

This is what happens when we surrender, when we lay down our lives, incomes, careers, hobbies, and habits before God. We die to ourselves, but in the process we find new life. We take up our life again after God has blessed it, and we live for him. We experience the power of the new life. This is part of what Jesus means when he says that to lose your life is to find it.

Moses began to experience a life-transforming God who liberated him to the design he had created. All that was required of him was surrender—an ongoing willingness to throw down his doubts, limitations, destructive tendencies, and deeply residing fears.

God asks the same question of us: "What is in your hand?" What is it that you hold onto? Are you willing to lay down the very things you clutch the tightest? Will you surrender them? Will you throw them down?

Once you have identified what holds you back, what pressures or issues keep you from moving from the despair of powerlessness to the risk of surrender?

Only when you surrender and then take up your life—the one of God's design—will you experience the full extent of God's healing work. Only then will you fully live the life he designed for you, the one you also desire in the deepest part of yourself.

4
NO MORE GAMES

A year after Bill's initial surrender to God, he faces a pen-and-paper inventory of his life. It has taken him years to begin and weeks to complete. Over time, his mother's stubborn tendencies to fight for him — her years of prayers, challenges, and steady forgiveness — have led him to living clean from meth, but what he sees in front of him now takes his breath away. He reads from his own carefully scripted lists of destructive habits, resentments, fears — a horrific number of pages recording the hurt and damage caused by his life. He seizes on the idea of a tornado to communicate the kind of rubble left in his wake.

Gauging by his level of personal pain at this point, Bill can see why he put off the fourth and fifth steps of recovery—honesty with yourself, God, and others. The evidence he has unearthed hurts like hell. At the same time, he acknowledges an understanding in his gut: the healing process hurts, and his lack of honesty has him stuck. He continues to engage in the lust of pornography, for example, but rationalizes that as long as he's clean, does it really matter?

Even deeper, at the places God has been at work in him, he realizes his soul is not well. The painful process of a personal inventory shuffles the rocks of the dark places of his past, and there is no telling what kind of creature may emerge. In the desperate hope that God will continue to work miraculously for and through him, he gathers together the pages of his past life and sets out, one by one by one, to make gracious amends for all the wrong he has done. Somewhere along the way, Bill feels himself running toward, and no longer away from, love.

A brutal honesty fuels our ongoing freedom. Along the important intersections of the road out—ditching denial, embracing dependence, and surrendering to God—honesty plays an integral role in the process. Yet honesty is so challenging. We have an amazing ability to shade the truth to our own desires or advantage. We justify. We rationalize. Particularly when it comes to our destructive issues, we have a tendency to lie to ourselves. We play games. We preface what we say with the concept of tomorrow. *Tomorrow I'll get help. Tomorrow I'll get honest. Tomorrow I'll get better.* And, in the hope of an elusive future, we are wrecked by a self-destructive past. Honesty requires a commitment to living well in the present.

Taking Inventory

In my own experience, the bridge moving me from tomorrow to today was built through taking a detailed personal inventory of my life. I had to ask hard questions of myself.

Do you have a difficult time admitting your own weaknesses? Do you like yourself? How have you hurt others, and what do you do about that? How much does fear — of failure, of rejection, of success — drive your life? How do you attempt to hide or protect yourself through habits or emotional distance? God desires love — and not fear — to steer your life.

The Exodus story reveals two opposing strategies for

life. Pharaoh abused power to coerce for selfish gain; God used power for the liberation of others. It was the slavery of fear versus the freedom to love.

God calls us to love. He asks that we risk the necessary honesty to move out of the life-draining grip of fear. When we get honest with ourselves we are ready to get honest with God and others. This honesty builds momentum on the road to freedom. Coming clean with God and others releases a healing power in our lives. But it starts with the inherent risks involved in letting out—and fully facing—the inner demons driving our external behaviors.

The sheer amount of bottled-up stuff in our lives is shocking. Several years ago we launched a website that allowed people a safe place to be completely honest. We challenged people to simply dump their junk. They could write anything they wanted—anonymously. There were no rules. I've never read anything quite so vulnerable and raw. People were pouring their hearts out online with no filter, no conventional layer of politeness, no religious faking it. There was an honesty to what they wrote that was both frighteningly brutal and pure—a cry for help in a question, a yearning, or a confession.

- *"I am addicted to the image of perfection at ALL times, even if it hurts those around me."*
- *"I turn to alcohol so I can feel NUMB, and all I really want is to feel LOVED."*
- *"I hate. I hate. I hate."*
- *"I was molested by my dad from the age of 13 to the age of 16, I never told anyone, not even my mom, and now it's tearing me apart."*
- *"I feel lost and abandoned by God."*

These kinds of questions, hurts, and confessions stand in stark contrast to what happens on the surface in most churches. There we're tempted to play the game and put on the show. As a pastor, I see it all the time — people wrestling with depression they don't understand, anger on the verge of being out of control, a lack of forgiveness toward a parent or spouse, sexual abuse endured as a child, adultery, an abortion, a fresh mark of self-injury on the arm, a pink slip. This is what is really going down, and often they're facing it alone — or not facing it at all.

We spend so much energy maintaining appearances and not enough dealing with the deeper internal issues driving our external behaviors. As a result, spiritual growth withers and lives get stuck in a holding pattern. Progress requires the ongoing confession of the brokenness of living in a world filled with sin.

In our contemporary culture, honesty often falls victim to "spin control." When we hear of the moral failings of celebrities like Tiger Woods, Jesse James, and John Edwards, the first response of the media usually goes something like this: "What can this person do to restore his or her image?" The larger question — can his or her character be restored? — is seldom addressed.

God does not want to improve our image but our lives. What he requires of us in the process of transformation is the honesty to admit our sin, recognize the damage it does, and move forward in faith that we might be able to love others better.

Honesty requires a full confession. As we see in the story of Bill, the temptation inherent in confession is an incomplete repentance. By failing to deal with the issue of pornography, he sacrificed the opportunity to move deeper and more honestly into his own life, which further connected his addictive behaviors to the root issue of a fear of intimacy. When he continued in honest confession, he learned to seek out the real—love—and not the substitute—lust. Ongoing honesty opens the door to God's grace that heals us.

It is tragic to me when we waste the opportunities God gives us to bring all of life into his light. James 5:16 challenges us in the right direction, "Therefore confess your sins to each other and pray for each other so that you may be healed." We are to pray for each other, but notice the condition for healing: *confession.* We'd rather camouflage our sins than confess them. There should be at least one person (your husband, wife, pastor, or a friend) you can share everything with, someone you know will love and accept you unconditionally. Ultimately, the result of this confession is healing.

Showdown

The story of Exodus sets up a showdown. In the one corner, you have Pharaoh, the king of a far-reaching empire, who stops at nothing to retain his power. In the other corner, you have the mysterious, virtually unknown God of a people under the pharaoh's enslavement. With each new encounter, God progressively revealed himself in his sovereignty.

The overarching significance of the plagues unfolds in God's showdown with the self-proclaimed incarnate god of the sun, Ra—the pharaoh himself. The plagues, presented in natural order, provided a dramatic platform for the showdown. The first two plagues—blood and frogs—were matched by the pharaoh's magicians, only to reveal that God was just getting warmed up.

Eugene Peterson wrote of God's progressive revelation of his power and sovereignty:

> By the third, the mosquito plague, the magicians were clearly out of their depth, no longer able to match Moses blow for blow. After the sixth, the boils plague, the magicians were not only bested, they were incapacitated, put out of action by the boils. We hear no more of them. The four final plagues, anchored by the death plague, settle the sovereignty issue decisively. Pharaoh is skunked.[1]

Pharaoh never found the courage to be honest with himself. And, as is the tendency of all dishonest men, he preferred to postpone surrender until tomorrow. Pharaoh had the opportunity to end the suffering. He simply had to let the Israelites go. Moses gave him the choice of when he planned to do so. Pharaoh responded with that little word again: "Tomorrow . . . I'll let them go tomorrow."

Following the seventh and eighth plagues, Pharaoh articulated remorse to Moses, saying, "Now forgive my sin once more and pray to the LORD your God to take this deadly plague away from me" (Exod. 10:17). His remorse, however, was short lived. As the plague faded, Pharaoh changed his mind and refused to let Israel go. At the core of the problem lies Pharaoh's dishonesty. Despite a crumbling kingdom, Pharaoh could not forfeit his power and—in the increasingly comic perception of his own control—refused to release the Israelites. He had multiple chances to change his life. His problem was that he didn't *really* want a changed life. All he wanted was a different situation.

It's the same with us. Confession means nothing if it does not come from a heart desiring God and his good and perfect will for our lives. And the best clue to the true condition of our hearts resides in how often we put off a necessary surrender until tomorrow.

What Lies Beneath

The process of taking a personal inventory uncovers what lies beneath our efforts of denial and dishonesty.

As Bill reads through his detailed lists of ways in which he has hurt others, his mind settles on one moment deep into his addiction to methamphetamines. Having moved back home, his life collapsing around him, he found a letter while pilfering through his mother's jewelry box. Seeing his name on the salutation, he began to read—his mother pleaded for him to get help while informing him of the chaos he had created within the family, including her near divorce. Bill remembers the stab of pain but, even worse, remembers ignoring his regret after finding the perfect ring to pawn for his next high.

"There was a point where I put pen to paper and laid everything out—the good, bad, and the ugly. I had to deal with my destructive habits, resentments, fears of living sober, and the pain and hurt I had caused my family and others. When I saw everything on paper I couldn't deny it anymore. I really didn't understand how powerless I was until I saw everything on paper."

Stop deceiving yourself and you will stop defeating yourself. I learned this in wrestling with anger. Anger has been a continual issue for me in my life, and I've wrestled with it again and again. Before I became a believer it was a serious limitation. I'd blow up in unpredictable ways. After surrendering to God I began to deal with it, and I made some good strides. But ten years later it came creeping back into my life in significant ways. I was too harsh with loved ones, too controlled by the moment.

Often our tendencies reemerge throughout our lives. When they do come back, the tendency to play games is huge. Rather than deal with my anger I told myself it was no big deal. I put it off and blew it off. After all, I was a Christian now and way better than I used to be, right? I kept playing games, but the people paying the price were those closest to me. Finally, one day I stood in the laundry room of our house staring at a hole I had just punched in the wall during a moment of anger. It was a massive wake-up call. I had to stop deceiving myself and reach out to God and others for help.

By taking inventory I learned a lot of my anger came from being overcommitted. I was traveling all the time and constantly stretched too thin at work. The result of this was a constant stress. My life was like a Coke bottle shaken up and ready to blow up at any moment. I had overcommitted to the point that if *anything* went wrong — a small delay due to car trouble, an extra errand my wife, Lori, needed me to run, a brief traffic jam on the freeway — it snowballed and *everything* went wrong. Because I failed to take into account that life is full of delays and detours, I concocted a recipe for disaster.

Often, we choose to play games because it's easier than tackling the difficult work of changing. I had to go back and completely reorganize my life. I made hard decisions and stopped a lot of things that I didn't really need to be doing. I still struggle with a tendency toward anger. But I've learned new skills in how to handle it. And so can you, if you are willing to get honest with yourself and look beneath the surface.

Are you a perfectionist? Are things ever good enough for you? Do you bury yourself under unrealistic expectations you can't meet, then try to find release in a relationship or a substance or whatever?

What about selfishness? Do you ever think of someone else's needs and concerns? Are you completely consumed with what you want?

Are you impatient?

Are you dishonest?

These are hard questions, but they are crucial. You may want to spend some time alone with a journal and with your thoughts to answer them. As you ask honest questions of yourself, don't despair. Jesus brings great hope. Confess and turn to him, and experience the power of God to love.

5
GRACE SPILLING OVER

I don't get it, but if you're into *The Price Is Right*, you are just into it. *The Price Is Right* has its own sort of cult following—including my wife.

Lori comes by her affection for the show genetically. Once Lori's great aunt Betty Sue went to the show before Bob Barker retired. They had shirts made that said, "All roads lead to Bob's The Price Is Right!" (And they actually *wore* them.)

They got second-row seats for the show and, sure enough, Betty Sue heard those magic words, "Come on down! You're our next contestant on *The Price Is Right*!" Believe me, Betty Sue made all those years of faithful viewing pay off. She guessed the right price of a riding lawnmower and won it. Then she played the Flip Flop Game (if you don't watch the show, I can't explain it) and won a vacation to Malaysia.

I confess: at this point in the show, I was almost as excited as Lori. I thought, "Way to go, Betty Sue! Please remember that we're related and that a riding lawnmower right now would be like getting underwear at Christmas. Malaysia, however, would be nice."

Then, if that wasn't enough, Betty Sue won the Big Wheel after a spin-off and made it all the way to the Showcase Showdown, where she finally lost. Still, for Betty Sue, the price was right more often than not.

The Bible speaks of the greatest price of all: to cover the cost of sin. The cost of sin is always so much greater than we first anticipate. At the same time the Scriptures tell us of the exorbitant price, they tell us it has already been paid by Christ's sacrificial death on the cross. Receiving his grace and forgiveness is one of the most important steps on the road to freedom.

For many of us, forgiveness of others comes more easily than forgiving oneself. Having survived myriads of abuse from others and our own destructive responses, our sense of self can feel so broken that shame becomes our name, an identity to hide behind. As one person confessed to me, "I don't feel like I deserve good things. I can never deserve God's grace, and evidently I am not smart enough to stop trying."

But here's the really good news about grace: on the road out to freedom, God is the one who never stops demonstrating again and again his powerful works of redemption.

RADICAL RISK

On the morning of a surgery that could take her father's life, Katie decides to be there, by the side of the man who sexually abused her.

By taking a step into her father's home, she ends an estrangement of years, a time necessary for her continued healing. As she reads her Bible on the morning of the surgery, Katie is reminded of how deeply God's grace continually rescues and restores her, and that forgiveness empowers the healing process.

The proof: she is here.

Here in the sense of being away from someplace and also

near. Away from the current of sexual and emotional abuse from a string of deeply broken father figures; away from the person she used to be, obsessively weighing her self-esteem by the number of pounds consumed in the passion of her eating disorder; and away from the girl who was determined never to take another step in the name of love.

And near . . . to her father and her Father.

She knows the risk. Even after forgiving her father, Katie sometimes hears an inflection of voice, the way he used to compliment her body, and she can't shake the feeling of danger.

As she reads through the Gospels in her father's house, she sees Jesus—one who pursues each of us in love, and whose offer of grace startles her once again. In the cycle of rubble from her own broken soul, marriage, relationships, and life, Katie learns to understand how hurt people hurt people, and she experiences the role forgiveness plays in the supernatural process of her own healing.

After years of shame connected to her abuse and even feeling responsible for it, she accepts deeply the gift of God's grace. She internalizes the fact that what happened was not her fault. She allows God's amazing mercy to heal her false perceptions of herself and her father.

She is here because of the Father to extend the same quality of grace to her father. She is here because of the places Jesus went for her—the cross and hell—so she could be free to face the obstacles blocking her own path, even if it means returning to the place where she experienced such a hell of suffering.

In the middle of reading through the book of John, her father, on the morning of his surgery, stumbles from his bedroom and asks what she is reading.

FREEDOM'S PRICE

Exodus powerfully pictures the price of freedom from sin, shame, and brokenness. As God unleashed his power through a series of supernatural miracles against Pharaoh, Israel stood on the cusp of freedom. With each consecutive plague, God moved closer to a real introduction of himself as the real ruler. In the ninth plague, God struck the sun against the self-proclaimed incarnate god of the sun, and darkness spread over the land. Pharaoh's reputation suffered damage. With the next plague, God went after Pharaoh himself by taking out his heir.

But this final plague, seen from a reverse angle, signifies something deeper: Israel's recreation and rebirth as a free people and a free nation. In Exodus 12:21–23 we read:

> Go at once and select the animals for your families and slaughter the Passover lamb. Take a bunch of hyssop, dip it into the blood in the basin and put some of the blood on the top and on both sides of the doorframe. Not one of you shall go out the door of his house until morning. When the LORD goes through the land to strike down the Egyptians, he will see the blood on the top and sides of the doorframe and will pass over that doorway, and he will not permit the destroyer to enter your houses and strike you down.

This passage describes what has come to be known as the Passover. God passed over every Israelite door that had blood on the doorframe. The event of the Passover marked the lives of the Israelites forever, memorialized in a holiday to begin each new year. Yet the liberation of God's people did not come without a price that had to be paid. The price was the blood of a lamb and, as we see in Exodus 12, an outpouring celebrated in the context of a feast. The price and the celebration went hand in hand to declare God moves miraculously in the lives of his people.

ISRAEL AND YOU

The same expression of salvation — a great price in the context of a great feast — occurs in the New Testament in the person and work of Jesus Christ. The spilling of the blood of the "Lamb of God" (John 1:29) found its celebratory feast in the bread and wine of communion. At the end of history, the feast will culminate in the greatest celebration of all: the wedding supper of the Lamb. From its inception, grace couples with celebration.

The parallels of Israel and the church began with a great movement of God for the freedom of his people. But when Jesus willingly shed his blood, he rescued us from something even more dreadful than slavery to a despotic and foreign king. He rescued us from the slavery of sin that ultimately ends in death.

At the same time God accomplishes his salvation, the obedience and faithfulness of his people is vitally important. If the Israelites had not spread the blood of the Passover lamb on their house, they would have died. God looked for blood on the door as a mark of obedience.

It's an odd limbo to navigate, but I have been there myself: believing that God's grace exists for everyone but me. For many believers, it seems that no matter what they do, they still can't shake the sense that past sins and mistakes condemn them. The inability to accept God's forgiveness first drove me to the performance treadmill, where I tried harder and harder to earn the love of God. And failing with my best efforts, I left plenty of room to wallow in pointless guilt.

Henri Nouwen believed the greatest temptation in life resides not in success, popularity, or fame, but in self-rejection. When a person believes the negative and condemning voices in the context of criticism or loneliness, he or she falls victim to the lie of condemnation and chooses to skip the recurring feasts of grace.[1]

Can you relate? In my own life, I considered my refusal of grace as somehow righteous, an acknowledgment of my deep brokenness. Only as God revealed my refusal as a cancerous form of self-pity and pride did I adjust my perspective enough to see the deeper reality.

In refusing grace, I was saying that Jesus was not enough and that his sacrifice needs to be greater. The death rattle of such pride finally brought me to the point where I could accept God's free gift of grace in the context of celebration and obedience.

GUILT AND SHAME

A vital difference exists between healthy and unhealthy guilt. Healthy guilt motivates us to amend relationships, make things right, and move toward health. It is focused on others more than on oneself. Unhealthy guilt often results in self-hatred. We condemn ourselves. We refuse to believe we can ever be accepted.

Shame debilitates. When I meet someone who wrestles with unhealthy guilt and forgiveness, I counsel them to read Psalm 51, which records David's prayer for forgiveness after committing the sins of adultery, murder, lying, and covering up. I challenge each person to read it and ask for forgiveness. Once finished, I tell them, "Don't ever ask God to forgive you for that sin again." For people who wrestle with shame, a pattern forms to bring up the same sins over and over again. I share what the Bible says: "He has removed our sins as far from us as the east is from the west" (Ps. 103:12 NLT). God has removed our sins from us as far as it is possible.

Confession of sin, of course, is healthy and a necessary part of daily biblical practice. However, constant confession of the same sin inhabits unbelief and not true confession, and the person is often left paralyzed on the road out to freedom.

If unhealthy guilt weighs you down read Romans 8 every day for the next two weeks. Really let the content sink into your life. I believe you will experience God's forgiveness anew: "So now there is no condemnation for those who belong to Christ Jesus. And because you belong to him, the power of the life-giving Spirit has freed you from the power of sin that leads to death" (Rom. 8:1–2 NLT).

This is the message of the good news: no condemnation! This message is for all who believe. So take heart and be encouraged. Grace is available to you solely because of who God is. Jesus sacrificed his life so that God could be both just in punishing sin and full of grace to you.

Grace On Grace

Katie smiles at her unshaven father, suspecting his question is nothing more than the small talk they have practiced for a lifetime—about the weather or the pets or the character in a movie, a camouflage for truths that he deeply buries.

But how can you be casual when asked about the gospel? In her own healing she has come to understand it as a grace spilling over, from one heart learning to embrace the grace of God to another. In the shadow of her father, she hesitates to answer.

Her father asks again, "What are you reading?"

When she blurts out, "The Bible," she expects a quick change of topic to a chance of thunderstorms, but he asks, "What are you reading about?"

"Jesus" is what she tells him. And from her own life, she speaks of the grace he offers, which frees her to deal with her own issues at the same time it releases her to take new steps toward others in love. She explains to him how she is healing.

A few minutes later, kneeling with her father in his prayer to receive Jesus, she sees the tears of a broken man fully loved. In this moment, she learns no matter how great the offense or abuse, the path of healing follows in the wake of coming to grips with the reality of forgiveness.

From Katie's life, grace spills over into her father's heart and, in spite of his terrible mistakes and sin, provides him with a new beginning through repentance. For both father and daughter, the shame disappears at the foot of the cross.

6
Hope on the Broken Road

Freedom is a process that begins when we admit we are powerless over our struggle and we need help. We look up to God, believing he listens, cares, and provides. We surrender to his will and get honest about our past and our mistakes. We depend on his spirit to give us strength. His grace is available and the price has been paid for our forgiveness, so we live in and celebrate each moment.

And then comes catastrophe. The road out is not a fast lane, and the journey to freedom stalls in potholes, dirt-road detours, and dead ends. Finding hope along a broken road requires the perseverance of faith.

Jennifer stands in the heat of a Texas afternoon on the porch of her childhood home, wondering why she came. Her friends had warned her, "Don't go back," but she's hoped against hope the relationship with her mom might be somehow repaired. After eighteen months of experiencing the supernatural power behind her sobriety, she reasons at least some small chance of reconciliation.

As she walks into an empty living room, trembling, the color of the carpet ignites a vivid flashback to her fifteenth birthday. As the images unwind, she sees herself in front of her mother, who is dressed for church and explaining once again why she can't go with them, even if it is her birthday and Easter Sunday. "God hates you because you are evil . . ." The words trail off as Jennifer runs out of the living room only to return with a prescription bottle of Motrin and 130 diet pills. In the slow motion of her recollection, Jennifer watches as she downs both bottles in front of her mom, and the last words she hears are her sister's, pleading with their mom to call an ambulance.

Now, as she waits for her mother, the memories continue to flood her mind. She sees herself on the living room sofa, sixteen and ninety-one pounds and almost always three sheets to the wind. She sees herself hooked on a concoction of ecstasy, acid, cocaine, and marijuana, and purging most of her meals, lying in a New Orleans hotel room on a morning after Mardi Gras. Hers is the face of an eighteen-year-old on a three-week binge, awakening to the realization she has used the last of the drugs, even the ones she was supposed to deal.

Jennifer hears a noise and plays with the idea of running out of the house and grabbing the first bus back to California, the residence of her recovery. But at just that moment, her mother interrupts the thought. As Jennifer makes her way into the living room, her mother announces that the basement bar is fully stocked.

Any real of hope of repairing the relationship with her mom quickly dissolves. As she returns home from a seven-mile bike ride to attend a recovery meeting, Jennifer's mother and sister mock her and offer her a glass of wine to help with the weariness. Within a few weeks, exhausted in her soul, Jennifer finds herself with a date at a bar ordering just one shot. The next thing she remembers is coming to, being given a case of champagne, and popping the corks until she blacks out again. Eighteen months of sobriety . . . gone.

Bricks without Straw

The experience of freedom inevitably engages setbacks and frustrations. After Moses first demanded to let God's people go, we read that Pharaoh made things harder on the Israelites: "That same day Pharaoh gave this order to the slave drivers and foremen in charge of the people: 'You are no longer to supply the people with straw for making bricks; let them go and gather their own straw. But require them to make the same number of bricks as before; don't reduce the quota. They are lazy'" (Exod. 5:6–8).

In the process of brick making, straw is a critical factor. By adding volume, strength, and structure to the mud-and-sand mix, straw allows the bricks to cure more quickly and hold together better. Making bricks without straw is like trying to build a cube out of Tinker Toys without using the little sticks that hold the discs together. You can do it, sort of, but not easily. Nor well.

On several critical moments on the road out to freedom, the book of Exodus demonstrates that the immediate path to freedom gets harder before it gets easier. The order of Pharaoh to nix the straw shows us that even slavery can get worse, and the temptation will continually arise to settle for a familiar life rather than one requiring the risks of dependence, faith, and perseverance. It is the same with the road out of habits and destructive tendencies. We often feel divided and torn because we want to be free but, at the same time, avoid too much additional pain. These vicious habits can divide and conquer us.

And that was the strategy of Pharaoh—to divide and conquer a people so that they would remain captive. We would be wise to pay attention to his tactics.

- First, he made their lives harder by demanding the same number of bricks without supplying the adequate components.
- Second, by appointing Hebrew foremen over the larger population of Hebrew slaves, Pharaoh pitted Hebrew against Hebrew.

Once again, Pharaoh's power strategy seems to make a great deal of sense. A divided Israel would be unable to accomplish their ultimate goal of freedom. He took their straw, and the people fell apart at the seams.

Sounds way too familiar, doesn't it? As we seek to deal

with our destructive habits and behaviors, we take the first steps out into the journey of freedom and face the ongoing realities of more pain. Often, the hurt is amplified by the fact that those we love — like the Hebrew masters — are the ones who inflict the pain. We are tempted to give up and retreat into the life we once knew.

On the road out, the destruction of our former lives sometimes catches up with us — past relationships corroded by our habits and struggles, and the weight of the baggage we carry towards others.

In my experience, the early days of recovery presented the most difficulties. When I first surrendered to God and began to experience freedom, all my problems did not disappear. To the contrary, I continually found myself in very tough situations. My life was no longer heading toward the crash. *The crash had happened. I'd survived.* Now what did I need to do to get to the next step?

I needed to:

- Distance myself from the friends I always partied with.
- Learn how to live sober.

- Discover how to face conflict, challenges, and other struggles without giving in to destructive patterns.

Handling all of that was a huge challenge. From the earthquake of my past, I had to deal with tons of emotional and relational rubble. I started the hard work of rebuilding, brick by brick.

At such difficult points, filled with exhaustion and hurt, we need to understand that, contrary to the power strategy of Pharaoh, God moves in love. He works mysteriously to empower the process of freedom. God saw Israel's absence of straw in another way: *as one more step toward freedom for his people.* In the familiarity of their lives of slavery, the additional hardship made life for the Israelites extreme enough that they *had* to move ahead. Exodus points us continually to a huge theme of the book: *the people would come to know the Lord.*

The real difficulty for each of us—and for Israel— resides in trusting that God has a plan and purpose, and that he has already orchestrated our deliverance.

In our lives things will get tough. We may feel like we are making bricks without straw, but God is teaching us to know and trust him. Unlike Pharaoh, God desires for us to grow and develop. Granted, it can be so frustrating when you make positive decisions and things seem to get worse or more confusing. But I've always flourished more through hard times than through good ones. When God takes your straw, it isn't because he wants you to remain a slave. It's because he wants you to take another step toward freedom.

FORGING AHEAD DESPITE DETOURS

Waking up after three days of nonstop drinking, Jennifer returns to her mother's house, stuffs her three backpacks, collects the eighty dollars remaining to her name, and buys a bus ticket back to California.

She prays repeatedly for the strength to continue and for enough of God's love to sustain her. Unexpectedly, at the oddest times and places, she finds the kindness of others — sleeping on the couches of friends, arms folded around her in prayers for continued recovery, a loan of a bicycle to ride to the two jobs she landed within a day of her arrival, and a request from a man in her AA group to watch his apartment while he serves a three-month sentence for a previous drunk-driving offense. In the resolution of her continuing surrender, she finds the growing peace and power of God to persevere in hope and faith. Things are hard emotionally, financially, and spiritually. But she is growing and walking the steps, however shaky, that lead out.

When things get harder it is normal to want to quit. We want to go back. We romanticize the past and remember what was good about the predictable routines of captivity. Fear causes us to lose our bearings. In the Sermon on the Mount, Jesus gave practical advice to his followers: "Therefore I tell you, do not worry about your life, what you will eat or drink; or about your body, what you will wear . . . Therefore do not worry about tomorrow, for tomorrow will worry about itself. Each day has enough trouble of its own" (Matt. 6:25, 34).

In our journey to overcome what holds us back, the essential focus is on today. What faces you right now? What choice do you need to make to take a positive step toward freedom? What worry do you need to give to God in the light of his promise that he will take care of you?

*Twenty years into sobriety, Jennifer recalls the great diffi-
culty and pain in leaving her mother's home so she could
continue her recovery. "I had to leave everything behind to
follow God's will and direction for my life. In the moment,
it is very difficult. You have to make a decision to give up
your own will and your control and take that plunge into
the ocean, usually having no idea what that means. That
has been my experience in surrendering. It means to have
faith in what you don't know and to trust in God for his
direction."*

When the road gets difficult, we all need words of
encouragement. As you face temptation, learn to meditate
on the Bible. I'll never forget hearing Charles Swindoll,
a well-known Christian writer and pastor, tell a personal story of resisting temptation. Following a speaking
engagement at a convention, two beautiful women got on
an elevator he was riding back to his room. Heading up,
they began to flirt with him. At one point one of them
asked, "Would you like a date tonight?" Swindoll was
tempted. He was worn out, and he was alone. But in the
moment, he heard over and over in his mind the words of

Galatians 6:7, "Don't be misled—you cannot mock the justice of God. You will always harvest what you plant" (NLT). Swindoll declined the young woman's offer.

Meditate on the Bible. Let its rich wisdom and insight live in your heart and mind. It will sustain you in the moments of temptation and remind you of the promises God gives us for each new day. Don't focus on yesterday or tomorrow; you have today. Settle into each moment. Trust God so you may make another step toward freedom.

7
MAKE IT RIGHT

As a young teenager, I was banned from all Sears stores until I was eighteen.

One day I had been leaving the store when a security guard grabbed my arm and said, "Excuse me, I need to know where you put the cassette tape."

I said, "I didn't put it anywhere. I don't know what you are talking about."

I lied.

He took me to a back room, where he searched me and didn't find anything. Then, just as his second search was ending, he felt something hidden just under my shirt. It was a cassette tape of the eighties band Dokken. I was busted.

When my father was called, I'm pretty sure he encouraged the store to call the police to teach me a lesson. In any case, the point was dramatically made: the police came, cuffed me, and walked me out the front door while everyone watched. They put me in a police car and took me to the station. I was terrified.

Even worse than my fear of jail, though, was facing my father. On the way home from the police station, he didn't say a word. The silence was deafening. Upon our return home, he asked me to sit down in the kitchen. He sat down next to me and looked out the window, again without saying a word. To this day, I remember the sound of the clock ticking. After what seemed like forever, my father finally spoke. "Jud, I don't understand why you would steal. You know better than that. You are better than that."

All I could say was, "I'm sorry," and offer to somehow make things right with my family and others. After that, my stealing days were over.

That day taught me that the heart of restitution begins with words that can be very difficult to speak: *I'm sorry.* In the years since, I have learned again and again that those words, combined with action to make practical amends, are life transforming. They are words of freedom.

Part of the reason for the difficulty of saying "I'm sorry" is that it requires us to focus on our own responsibility and not the behavior of others. We all get hurt. In my own life, I can think of a couple of people who betrayed my trust and deeply wounded me. I remember the all-consuming anger and bitterness I felt toward them for a long time. Most of us could develop long lists of ways we have been treated unfairly or suffered because of the words or actions of others.

- My father was emotionally absent.
- My uncle molested me.
- My mother abandoned our family.
- My boss exploited me.
- My best friend betrayed me.
- My mortgage company ripped me off.
- My children aren't grateful for the sacrifices I've made for them.
- My God has led me into a desert to die.

We've all been hurt, we've all been burned, and we've all been wronged. And the temptation is always to think, "I'll say I'm sorry when he says he's sorry."

The temptation of blame resides in two powerful psychological realities. One may seek to shift *all* of the responsibility for the pain to the one who has hurt them and attempt to inflict at least an equal amount of suffering on that person. And the deadly reality plays itself out: hurt people seek to make others pay for their pain.

Part of the healing resides in turning the tables. How many lists would your name appear on in regard to hurting others? Each of us damages people and relationships. Each of us makes blunders that hurt others. Don't play the blame game — seek to make amends for your own mistakes. If you do, I guarantee you a surprise along the way.

RESTITUTION

Throughout the desert wanderings, God established a series of commands to help the Israelites say, "I'm sorry"—not just uttering the words, but combining the vocabulary with acts of restitution. Through a series of if-then scenarios recorded in Exodus 22, God established a loving process for making things right when someone is wronged.

It's clear how seriously God stresses the importance of restitution. In some instances, amends are required beyond the original offense. A person caught stealing is asked to pay back several times the value of what was stolen. Even more surprising is that God sometimes requires amends even if the crime was not intended. Exodus 22:6 records, "If a fire breaks out and spreads into thornbushes so that it burns shocks of grain or standing grain or the whole field, the one who started the fire must make restitution."

Although a fire breaking out defines a particular circumstance for restitution, it also serves as a deeper picture of the way damage occurs. Most of the time, we do not consciously desire to hurt the ones we love. Sometimes things just get out of control. We don't always mean to neglect our children by allowing the pressure of work to take control of our time. We don't really intend some of the words we say to a spouse in a moment of anger. We rarely see the blind spots we use to protect ourselves and manipulate others.

By developing codes for restitution, God acknowledges the terrible risks we take in wounding others for personal gain. Restitution is the process of making loving attempts to reverse the damage of hurt caused either intentionally or unintentionally. Healing resides in the motivation to repair a relationship in the name and power of love.

Ultimately, God's model of restitution fully engaged in the cross of Jesus. Jesus made restitution on our behalf for something he did not do. Furthermore, he is our supreme example of repairing relationships that have been broken. If we embrace him, then we must also embrace a lifestyle of restitution.

AMENDS AND FORGIVENESS

Following their son's soccer game on a bright Las Vegas afternoon, Shaun hands his Blackberry to his wife without thinking. Opening the browser, she finds her husband's last page—an online advertisement for a paid escort. When he rips the phone from her hands, his truck swerves across the right lane, and they nearly crash. She begs and screams at him to hand it over, but he holds on.

At home, Shaun locks the door of the bathroom and erases all the critical history and files necessary to maintain most of his innocence. As he does so, his wife, screaming in anger, throws framed wedding photos against the bathroom door.

A day or so later, Shaun feels sick and suicidal and wants to confess but can't imagine how he could keep from losing his family if his wife discovers the full truth. In a basement room, he descends into the self-hatred found in the depths of shame.

In a different room of the same house, Lynette's carefully designed plan to build a family totally different from the one she has known—free from abuse and addiction—crumbles around her. Struggling in a depression triggered by new discoveries of her husband's infidelities, she realizes a terrible history is repeating itself with the same emotional foundation of fights, secrets, lies, and addictions. The education degrees, good jobs, and a landscaped house are exposed as a façade, and Lynette wonders what—if anything—lies behind the disguise. Once again, she falls apart in feelings of failure.

At this point in time, Shaun and Lynette share a broken

marriage, shattered histories, and a deep longing for change without any hope of ever doing so. They feel alone in the desert, both literally and figuratively.

Feeling powerless, they both seek help. Shaun is diagnosed as a person in the grip of sexual addiction, and Lynette is asked to work through the issues of codependency. They attend a recovery meeting at Central Christian Church and, despite their initial horror of bringing God into these affairs, tap into power through continuing surrender neither of them could imagine.

Lynette experiences both a heartbreaking loss and an unrelenting obsession. She remembers the depths to which she plummeted late one night well after her children and husband (in another room) fell asleep. Sitting on the floor of their bedroom, hours into her continuing search of websites and bank accounts for more of her husband's secrets, she listened to the swirl of voices repeating the same questions in her head: who has he been with, what have they done, and how could he do that to me? Exhausted and shaky and confused, the tears began to flow and she made a vow to stop hurting herself. She has more than enough pain to go around without self-inflicted wounds.

On an evening months into their recovery, Shaun rehearses the words he plans to say to his wife. As they both work through the Celebrate Recovery principles and steps, Shaun understands the importance of making amends, but how do you convince someone, after a thousand times of saying you're sorry, that this time you really mean it? And, if Lynette even listens, how will he do everything in his power to make it right? Even though he doesn't really have the answers to those questions, and he fears he may put his marriage in jeopardy, Shaun trusts in God. He asks his wife if they could talk after putting their children to bed.

On the living room couch, he starts by losing control, weeping uncontrollably. Through his sobs, he apologizes for not only his betrayal, but for all the other terrible ways the deception resulted in her pain. He lists all he can remember, and it takes him a while. He stresses that there was nothing she could have done or said to have changed his choices. And then he waits.

And waits.

It's not that Lynette doesn't want to respond—she just can't find the words to acknowledge the supernatural reality she feels in the moment. In her own healing process, she has experienced the love and grace of God, which has freed her to work on her own issues instead of trying to fix her husband through her own anger, shame, and obsession. As she submits her husband in prayer to the care of God, she discovers beneath her rage a deep sadness over losing her husband and best friend. After Shaun's confession, it takes Lynette a little time to do the calculation that he has not left one hurt uncovered.

In forgiving him, she thanks him for his apology and the healing gift that it is to her.

Lynette's forgiveness marks a turning point in the life of Shaun, a man who had descended into the pits of deceit and shame. In his sexual addiction, Shaun rationalized sex with prostitutes on the basis of emotional disconnection, and now, through the door of forgiveness, he experiences—and longs for—intimacy. In his wife's love he sees the love of Jesus. For a person who has already condemned himself to a life without love, it feels to Shaun like a resurrection.

Shaun works hard to make things right. He accepts that it will take time for Lynette to fully trust him again. He knows this will mean vulnerability with his cell phone and e-mail, with his time and privacy, but he embraces it. No more secrets. No more lies. He begins to restore the relationship one step at a time through depending on Jesus, facing his own struggle, seeking the help of others, and maintaining transparency with his wife.

A year or so later, Shaun and Lynette renew their marriage vows on a beach in Southern California. As she looks into the faces of fifty or so close friends and family, she recognizes a woman who once told her that she would come to celebrate the circumstances leading to their recovery. She smiles at the thought. In the earthquake of a marriage broken by infidelity and addiction, she could see nothing except pain for the longest time, but now she begins to see what the woman meant. Through a desperation leading to God, an honesty requiring grace, an ongoing surrender marked by dependence, the options narrow to two: faith or self-destruction. In the seeking and giving of forgiveness, they renew their vows with God at the center.

The Urgency of Forgiveness

The kind of forgiveness demonstrated by Shaun and Lynette occurs over time, a process requiring the repeated use of the *S* and *F* words: "I'm sorry" and "I forgive you." Sometimes people forgive too quickly and easily without first really grieving and working through the process with God. If anger or some other negative emotion has been there for years, get some help. Don't be afraid of Christian counseling. Work through those issues, because there is tremendous freedom on the other side.

Jesus taught that there is a great urgency about forgiveness. He said that reconciliation is important enough to drop whatever you are doing to seek forgiveness and healing within a relationship (Matt. 5:23–24). Sometimes you have to put one foot in front of the other and just do it, even though you do not feel a desire to do so or would rather excuse yourself through the blame game.

An important step in your journey to freedom is to stop and make a list of people you have harmed in your life. As you make this list, also think of those who have harmed you. Be willing to offer forgiveness—and seek forgiveness too. Be willing to take those risks and say, "I'm sorry" and "I forgive you."

8
LET GOD FIGHT FOR YOU

When Jeff sets up his new residence as a homeless man on a curb halfway down the hill from the bus stop, he calculates in his head the distance necessary for a driver to see him then stop and pitches what remains of his possessions on that precise spot. He needs a way out if all else fails him.

Surrendering to the last of his drugs, an IV fuse of cocaine and heroin, Jeff lifts one final desperate prayer: "Please end the pain." He prays to Jesus, but he isn't certain why.

Before his parents' divorce and his plunge into emotional and physical poverty, Jeff was drawn to the reality of Jesus. As a child and in-training altar boy, he remembers spending hours in the dark of a lonely altar searching the face of Jesus *and wondering why a man would willingly put himself in the place of such suffering.*

Years later, on the day of release from another rehabilitation sentence, Jeff asks Jesus to save him. Two hours later he is back on the street with another needle in a pockmarked vein. At this moment of retreat back into his habits, which would last for decades, Jeff feels the reality of a love that pursues him rather than the other way around. Helpless addict that he is, he understands Jesus as somehow fighting for him in a way he can never understand.

At the same time he lifts another simple prayer to Jesus—"Help"—he practices the sequence again, just as he envisions: step, step, step, step, a loud horn, squealing brakes, and then a thud. An end to his pain.

DON'T PANIC

In the story of Exodus, God cast Israel as the ultimate underdog. He chose Moses, a shepherd and murderer, to lead a captive people into a showdown with the king of a spreading world empire. The point of the narrative: God's glory remains unstoppable. Redemption works in his power alone, and his grace allows us to receive it.

You are asked to believe.

Imagine the odds against the underdog Israel. Thousands and thousands of troops in a state-of-the-world war machine descended in chariots and horses while the raging Red Sea blocked the only escape. Can you imagine the pressure?

Exodus 14:13–14 picks up the story: "Moses answered the people, 'Do not be afraid. Stand firm and you will see the deliverance the Lord will bring you today. The Egyptians you see today you will never see again. The Lord will fight for you; you need only to be still."

On their journey out of Egypt, God led his people into an apparent trap. Outside of a supernatural work of God, there existed no hope. And Moses' answer: be still and God will fight for you.

In other words, don't panic.

Be serious.

A while back someone e-mailed me a news item about what to do just in case you are ever in the heart of the Amazon and manage to get yourself swallowed by an anaconda (the largest of snakes, often growing up to thirty-five feet long and capable of swallowing whole a four-hundred-pound animal). These are the steps you should take:

- If you are attacked by an anaconda, don't run. The snake is faster than you are.
- Lie flat on the ground. Put your arms tight against your sides and your legs tight against one another.
- Tuck in your chin.
- Do not panic, but the snake will begin to nudge and climb over your body.
- After the snake has examined you it will begin to swallow you from the feet in, always from the feet in. Permit the snake to swallow your feet and ankles. Do not panic.
- The snake will now begin to suck your legs into its body. You must lie perfectly still. This will take a long time.
- When the snake has reached your knees, slowly and with as little movement as possible, reach down to get your knife and very gently slide it into the snake's mouth between the edge of its mouth and your leg. Suddenly rip upwards, severing its head.

Don't panic? Give me a break.

The Glory of God

Israel cried out to God in panic: "Was it because there were no graves in Egypt that you brought us to the desert to die? What have you done to us by bringing us out of Egypt? Didn't we say to you in Egypt, 'Leave us alone; let us serve the Egyptians'? It would have been better for us to serve the Egyptians than to die in the desert!" (Exod. 14:11–12).

Again, we run into a reality of choosing the certainty of slavery over the promise of freedom. Israel was a people who should've known better. They witnessed a series of devastating plagues that brought Egypt to its knees, but still they found it difficult to believe. Through Moses, God told the people to stand still and watch what he would do. Let there be no mistake about it: the redemption of his people and world resided in his inevitable power and movement of his glory.

The command to not be afraid and to stand still is often used in Old Testament military scenes. In this case, it was as if the battle lines were drawn. Israel was on one side and Egypt on the other. Israel was facing an overwhelming Egyptian army with superior military technology.

The only chance of victory belonged to God.

Be still so God alone gets the glory.

God's glory is intimately connected to our deliverance. God's plan intertwines with the details of human life. Way too often we forget that when God tells us to wait, he doesn't do so to burn some time but to reveal his supernatural activity in the context of our lives. He tells us to wait, so we can clearly see him at work.

God loves the patient faith of an underdog.

Do you ever feel like an underdog? Like nothing ever seems to go your way, and life seems difficult at best, even impossible at times? Take heart. The good news of the work of Jesus, staked in the suffering of the cross, is that the odds have been reversed. In the end, the underdogs win.

I admit to a fondness for the *Rocky* movies. After the first time Sylvester Stallone yelled out, "Yo, Adrian," I bought a punching bag and hung it in the shed behind our house in the unlikely hope of becoming a boxer. I was lucky enough to screen the final movie of the series, *Rocky Balboa*, with a small group of people who got to attend with Stallone. When asked about biblical themes running through the movies, Stallone pointed to the first scene of the first movie, which opened on a painting of

Jesus. The camera then panned down to reveal an old church transformed into a rundown boxing ring. As Balboa slugged it out from the bottom of his life and career, Jesus stood above him, with the word "Resurrection" on the wall behind the ring.

Rocky had a destiny to fulfill, and even though he was a broken guy down on his luck — the symbol of the ultimate underdog — God was not finished with him or the final storyline.

Like Rocky and Israel, we must act and not just wait. In the paradox of the gospel, redemption finds its path along the line of an active faith. Check out the sense of irony in God's response to the plea of Israel: "Then the Lord said to Moses, 'Why are you crying out to me? Tell the Israelites to move on'" (Exod. 14:15). Moses already knew what to do. Go before the Red Sea, lift up his staff, and get this thing moving.

In Scripture, we always experience the tension between waiting and action. Some people say they wait on the Lord when they intend their own laziness. There lies a great temptation of failing on one side or another.

If you have an issue with bitterness or anger toward

another person, you don't avoid a conversation in favor of staying in your closet to pray. God says, "I'll work and you can watch me work, but you need to participate through faith in what I am doing."

The Israelites ran as hard as they could to the very end of the Red Sea with the Egyptians in pursuit. And then God rescued them. The sea swallowed the Egyptians.

This is the great salvation moment in the history of Israel. The first time the word *save* is used in the Bible occurs here in Exodus 14. The Hebrew word is reserved almost exclusively for the work of God. It is through his grace that we get in on it.

PARTY TIME

On the other side of the Red Sea, a free people celebrated. They sang out to God:

> I will sing to the LORD,
>> for he is highly exalted.
> The horse and its rider
>> he has hurled into the sea.
> The LORD is my strength and my song;
>> he has become my salvation.

He is my God, and I will praise him,
> my father's God, and I will exalt him. (Exod. 15:1–2)

Moses began the song with the first person ("I") and quickly shifted his attention to God. The Lord had won the victory, and his people celebrated the fruits of that victory.

The song focuses on God's power and mighty deliverance. When God's people see his mercy, the result is elation, praise, and joy. Israel had seen God move. They couldn't help but shout for joy. God is the central figure of the song because of what he has done.

The party reverberates into eternity. Revelation 5:9 declares Jesus worthy of praise because he "purchased men for God from every tribe and language and people and nation." That opens up the invitation to God's party to all of us.

God's activity on our behalf cannot fully be expressed or experienced except through worship and praise. When we celebrate our victories—whether it's another day sober or a restored relationship—our joy does not focus on what we have done, but rather on what Christ has done on our behalf.

Start the party now. Thank God for the fact you're on the journey to know him better—the journey to be free. Celebrate the truth that Jesus promises about the freedom he brings: If the son sets you free, you are free indeed.

On the curb downhill from the bus station, Jeff takes one step, and then another, and then another with the same precision he has practiced during two hopeless years on the street. Just after taking his last step, he runs into an invisible object that knocks him backward, away from the path of the bus. It feels to him like walking into a sliding-glass door. As Jeff rises, both stunned and angry, he cries out to God in the rage of his helplessness. "I can't take this anymore! Either help me or kill me, God, because I am broken and at the end of myself!"

From a place deeper down than his rage, Jeff senses a power moving through his powerlessness, beyond his fear and hate, and in his surrender a spark nestles into his soul. Finding his way that evening to the Las Vegas Rescue Mission for a bite to eat, God places in his path a mission resident who leads him into a Steps Recovery program.

He records the moment to continually celebrate the work of God, who does for him what he can't.

Two years into his sobriety, Jeff experiences a life of joy and purpose previously unimagined. He points to his personal paraphrase of the text of Psalm 107 to describe his new life of thanksgiving:

Let's give thanks to the Lord for his unfailing love and his wonderful deeds for men, for he satisfies the thirsty and fills the hungry with good things. Some sat in darkness and the deepest gloom, prisoners suffering in iron chains for they rebelled against the words of God and despised the counsel of the Most High, so he subjected them to bitter labor; they stumbled, and there was no one to help. Then they cried to the Lord in their trouble, and he saved them from their distress. He brought them out of darkness and the deepest gloom and broke away their chains. Let them give thanks to the Lord for his unfailing love and his wonderful deeds for men.

After God's remarkable and supernatural intercession, Jeff acts. He works through each of the steps in his recovery program, seeks to make amends to the people he has hurt, and takes seriously his responsibility to move forward in his recovery. But this time the motivation behind his actions is different from a lifetime of similar efforts to find healing. What was missing, Jeff says, was the knowledge of the love of God. As God continues to accomplish a recovery beyond Jeff's own power, he understands God does so out of love. And it blows him away. Out of that love, he finds himself not so much acting on his own behalf but responding to God's love by extending grace to others. As he comes to grips with God's forgiveness, he responds by forgiving himself and others.

Jeff now helps lead the recovery program at our church and has been involved with ministry to the homeless. "I have a relationship with Jesus today that is priceless. I know this journey through recovery is a life-long process and I still battle against my own desires to serve myself. But what's different today is that I know I'm not alone. I know God loves me. When times get rough, which they do, I go to God. I contact people, share how I feel, and work through situations, not run from them. My life has meaning. I have peace, not pain, and I've become willing to let God work through me to reach out and help the one who is suffering."

9
DITCH THE LONER ROUTINE

Mark's plan to do a Nicolas Cage and leave Las Vegas runs smoothly to a certain point. The idea of a man drinking himself to death takes on a strange appeal for Mark, who is forty-two and feels he has no options. Leaving a woman who still loves him and two children who consider it no big loss, Mark checks into a Las Vegas apartment and—just like in his plan—furnishes it with nothing other than a sleeping bag and refrigerator. In his mind, as the police kneel over him, he expects one of them to say that it's just another suicide stiff.

Sick to death of the carnage from decades of addiction, running from everything and everyone, Mark sits night after night in his apartment, back leaning against the bedroom wall, drinking until he blacks out. In the mornings, when he comes to, he does not recognize where he is or, more often, thinks to himself, Damn, I'm still here and alone.

ARMS HELD UP

God does not intend for us to live our lives in isolation. We are not designed to be loners. On their way out of Egypt, God's people lived and moved as a community. After encountering the Amalekites, who vowed Israel's destruction, the people teamed together for battle in a way that expressed their need for each other and God. As Joshua led the troops out in war, Aaron and Hur stayed with Moses. Exodus 17:10–12 reads:

> So Joshua fought the Amalekites as Moses had ordered, and Moses, Aaron and Hur went to the top of the hill. As long as Moses held up his hands, the Israelites were winning, but whenever he lowered his hands, the Amalekites were winning. When Moses' hands grew tired, they took a stone and put it under him and he sat on it. Aaron and Hur held his hands up — one on one side, one on the other — so that his hands remained steady till sunset.

We cannot win on our own. We can't find freedom alone. Even with God on his side, Moses needed others to walk with him and hold his arms up. He needed others who would encourage and pray with him. So do we.

Becoming free and staying free from the stuff that holds us back is never an isolated thing. It happens in community with the help and encouragement of others. One of the most important ways to stay free is to set strong relational ties with people who are positive and life giving, who encourage you to make wise decisions and cheerlead you when you do.

When I realized my life was crazy and unmanageable, I reached out to God, but I would have never made it if it wasn't for a small group of people at my local church who loved and cared for me. God used them to save my life. That was more than twenty years ago, but the same principles hold true for me today. I stay free and keep growing because of the relationships in my life. The small group of people who challenge me and walk with me are invaluable to my personal and spiritual growth.

The point of desperation brings about the possibility of community. People who are helpless are often more willing to seek out another's help. Believers form a community united by their brokenness but also dedicated to love, support, help, and advocate for one another. They share a faith that human beings can change and grow in the grace, love, and power of Jesus.

I love the imagery of the arms of Moses extended by hands on his right and left, and the dependence of Moses—on God and his brothers. For me, it's the story of community.

Seeing Jesus

When Mark shows up at a recovery group, Sherman recognizes the look of a beaten person—suicidal, isolated, given over to shame and bitterness. A few years ago, it was his own life. Sherman gives Mark the kind of hug that takes your breath away and, before Mark knows it, he is leading him in a prayer to accept Jesus into his life. A sense strikes Mark then, as it has at critical points during his suicide plan, that maybe there's another way.

As they talk with one another afterward, Sherman tells Mark he's not alone and shares the story of how he finally said "enough." After his own suicide attempt and weeks into his sobriety, when his ride back from an AA meeting cancelled, Sherman called an old friend, a cook for his former dealer, who drove him to a crystal-meth lab. After nineteen years of drug addiction—eight caught in the insanity of smoking meth—Sherman smelled the meth on the way back from the bathroom and knew how much he wanted it. At the moment he feared for his soul, he ran outside and began praying, "Dear God, please help me. I don't want this anymore, and I don't want to lose my little girl."

When the dealer came out to talk with him, Sherman told him no. Back home in the shower, Sherman got sick like he used to with the drugs and questioned what was different this time from the other thousands of times he tried to say no before.

It was God, Sherman tells Mark, and Mark knows what he means.

Truth be told, Mark doesn't care too much for Sherman initially. This pushing Jesus right in his face and telling him he needed to say this prayer—it makes Mark dislike him because he feels an exclusive claim on loud-mouthed arrogance. At the same time, Mark feels this mysterious draw—a spark in Sherman's eye—to keep showing up for something that just might be there.

Sherman becomes his sponsor, and there are some days Mark wishes he could talk about baseball or the weather. Working through the Steps Recovery program, Sherman seeks to engage the most difficult challenge of recovery—helping one to see the truth about oneself. He challenges Mark to do the hard work—repentance, seeking forgiveness, making amends, and telling the truth—all in the context of the grace of Jesus, whom Mark genuinely begins to see in the love of Sherman. In the process of working through the issue of making amends for his lifestyle of addiction, Marks meets with Sherman in a park and reveals a number of dark secrets.

Over and over he hears from Sherman and a community of church around him: good news, dude—Jesus has you covered.

On the evening of his baptism in front of thousands of people, Sherman comforts Mark, who is nervous about standing in front of such a large crowd. Sherman tells him it's not about the crowd or, for that matter, about Jesus this time. "It's about you," he says. "Through your baptism, you are telling the world of the grace of God to redeem a life."

Sherman baptizes him and when Mark surfaces from under the water, instead of the face of Sherman, he sees Jesus.

A few seconds later, Sherman looks at Mark with that overly confident smile and asks him, "You saw Jesus, too, didn't you?"

KEEP SHOWING UP

Sometimes when people make a decision for Christ, they corner me and say, "I've made this decision. I've been baptized. What do I need to do now?" When I don't have time to give them the long answer, I give them the three-word short version: "Keep showing up." Some people protest, wanting something more specific like a training course or a commitment to a year without chocolate. Do you know what I've learned? Life really is 90 percent about showing up. Hebrews 10:25 argues for the reality of community, "Let us not give up meeting together, as some are in the habit of doing, but let us encourage one another—and all the more as you see the Day approaching." The early believers stayed connected to one another.

So, keep showing up. Keep showing up before God in prayer and study. Keep showing up with encouraging friends. Keep showing up at church. Because when you show up, God moves. He is going to work in your life in community, and in a way that you could never do on your own.

As a celebration of continuing recovery, Mark and Sherman's community group rents a cabin on Panguitch Lake in Utah. Nine adults—and a bunch of children—gather for the second straight year. Having spent at least three years together, the group comes together in ways that have become natural to them. Recovering addicts, previously isolated and alienated, share with one another ongoing struggles, fears, and hopes. They are each other's uncles and aunts, and they have learned what it means to have a brother or sister in the world too. Against great odds, by the grace and power of God, they share a deep response of worship and wonder together. They continue to build a track record of showing up for one another.

On the second day of the retreat—Independence Day—Mark feels the need to clear his head following a dinner together. As he fires up an ATV, Sherman happens along and asks Mark, "Mind if I join you?"

Just before the road becomes a path into the woods, Sherman requests a trade of four-wheelers; he prefers the manual transmission. They make the exchange, and Mark watches as his friend heads out first. As Sherman begins to climb the short uphill grade, he glances back with a look that says he's not going to make it. As if in slow motion, Mark watches him go up, watches the four-wheeler overturn and spill Sherman fifteen feet to the ground.

When Mark reaches him, Sherman says, "I'm messed up." He can't move his arms or legs. His face is in the dirt and he can't breathe, so Mark digs a hole beside his mouth and nose. With the air he can manage, Sherman begins to pray. "Please, God, help me to be okay."

After the ambulance leaves, Mark stays behind with the police. When the necessary papers are completed, the police leave and Mark stands alone in the middle of the darkening woods. He wonders what has happened. He feels the isolation, fears his best friend might be paralyzed below the neck or dying, and he yells out, "Where were you, God?" More than the fear, he is shaken by his inability to do anything to help. He prays for ways to love his brother Sherman.

Hours later, shortly before his transfer from Utah to a Las Vegas hospital, C-scan tests are conducted on Sherman, who becomes nauseous. Strapped down to the table, unable to move anything below his neck, Sherman turns to his friend Mark and asks him to sing a song.

"Blessed Is the Name of the Lord" is the first song that comes to Mark's mind, and it's what he sings to his friend. In the shared community of pain, hope, and dependence, Sherman can't feel Mark's hand on his, but he knows it is there.

In the wake of Sherman's accident, Mark often feels powerless to help much, but he continues to practice the words of his mentor critical to his own recovery: "Just keep showing up." By sitting in hospital waiting rooms and phoning the rehab facilities and showing up whenever he can with a joke, story, word of encouragement, or a prayer, Mark provides healing to his friend in ways he never understands.

10
GUARD YOUR HEART

Okay, I admit—I'm a closet reality-TV fan.

It's not an admission I'm proud of. I mean, come on, reality TV is shallow, it's a waste of time, and it's mindless . . . but I *like* it! Actually, my wife watches and I get drawn in. When a reality show is on, I'll sit in the living room with my computer as if I'm working, positioning myself in such a way that I can see the TV. Once I'm hooked, I'm addicted for the run of the show. One of the lowest moments in my adult life happened when I moved an appointment so I could get home to see the final episode of *The Bachelorette*.

You kind of lose respect for me as a pastor, don't you? One of my favorite reality shows is *American Idol*. I love to see ordinary people whose whole lives get changed by the show. And I'm a voter. I call in my picks just like millions of other Americans.

The reality for Americans is that we love our idols.

GOOD IDOLS ARE THE WORST

An idol from a biblical standpoint is anything that takes our attention away from worshiping the one true God. Whether it is people, stuff, hobbies, or addictions, we are often quick to place things in our lives before God. When we do, we begin to drift from the path to freedom. If we are going to stay free, it's crucial to guard our hearts and keep God first.

For the longest time, Molly's recovery is fueled by fear. She stalls on taking a personal inventory because of her certainty that she couldn't stand the pain — too much heartbreak, rubble, and litter of lives. Sober for eight years, she continues to build a recovery driven by fear. A head-on collision with another drunk driver tends to draw a conclusion that there's a deeper problem. But the shame, visiting memories of the times she sold herself for drugs, and the broken lives in the wake of her past are too much for her. She believes it would kill her to have to go there.

So, even as she enters ministry as an assistant to those in recovery, she takes the remaining steps of her recovery on the thin backs of good idols — in order: sobriety, ministry, food, and her relationship with her husband.

And it's her husband who is now causing the problem. As he enters into a seventy-two-week chemotherapy treatment for exposure to Agent Orange in the Vietnam War, her once-caring husband has retreated into a despondency resulting in abusive and delusional behavior. Her constant fear that she will find him dead in the basement leads her to eat everything in sight. When a friend suggests she revisit the idea of a personal inventory, she responds that it's her husband's fault.

Molly thinks she is doing okay — eight years sober, giving herself for the cause that saves her life. And then comes the chaos of her husband's chemotherapy and the toxic sludge he leaves in her life. Fearing his suicide, she breaks down, eats up, and finds it necessary to take a break from her ministry job. Molly watches each of her idols crumbling before her in slow-motion death.

She seeks help and enters another Steps Recovery program. When she finally summons the courage to take a personal inventory of her life, the pain she experiences is no less than she imagined and feared. At one point, she calls a friend to ask for help but manages only a series of uncontrollable sobs. Molly believes she won't hold up in the overwhelming flood of pain and regret but understands that continued healing resides in a renewed perspective about her relationship with God. Out of his love, God supplies the power to change. She is finally willing to bank her life on it.

When she returns home after weeping into the phone with her friend, Molly sees her husband differently. Instead of a monster degrading her with his moods and post-traumatic spells, she sees a man she loves struggling against his own issues. She no longer insists upon his growth before hers and grants him the freedom to suffer alone. She no longer accepts responsibility to fix his pain. She checks into a weight-loss program and loses sixty pounds and no longer indulges in the requirement of food to numb her pain. By working through her past, seeking forgiveness, and making amends when possible, she begins the process of replacing fear with love.

At one point during her husband's chemotherapy treat-

ment, Molly receives a text message in her home office—from her husband sitting in the living room: why aren't you checking in on me? From the days of her codependence, overwhelmed by her husband's abusive and often delusional behavior, she recognizes the temptation to fall deeper into guilt and feelings of helplessness. Instead she walks straight into the living room, looks him in the eye, smiles, and says, "How am I supposed to get better if you don't give me the room to do so?" In the process of her own recovery, she marks the moment of transition into truly loving others, without staking her own value on the results. She eats less, prays more, and finds increasing freedom in God.

DRIFTING FROM THE PATH

The Israelites were free. They had crossed through the Red Sea. They had received commandments from the very heart of God for how to live their lives. These guys would never drift from the path of God's freedom, right?

Exodus 32 paints the story of Israel's readiness to craft idols to replace God on a very short notice. Moses had been on the mountain for forty days and nights as he received the revelation of God's law and tabernacle, the place he promised to inhabit with his presence. One of the lowest points in the Exodus story follows Moses' mountaintop experience with God. Apparently, Israel suffered from corporate attention deficit disorder.

Israel was ready to be like the other nations they'd heard about: they wanted to worship an idol. They forgot to take an honest inventory of their journey with God. As a consequence, manna in the desert became boring. Water coming out of rocks seemed passé. God guiding them with miraculous signs in the sky looked pyrotechnic. That Red Sea bit was impressive when it happened, but those Egyptians really were overrated as chariot drivers. In its corporate crafting of a hand-made idol, Israel denied the power, grace, and love of God setting them free.

Who was this God who led them into a desert, and where was he now? Wasn't it time to worship a god with some kind of physical form, who could be depended upon to show up on a better timetable? Even Moses' brother, Aaron, yielded to the demand of the people. Exodus 32:4 picks up the story: "He took what they handed him and made it into an idol cast in the shape of a calf, fashioning it with a tool. Then they said, 'These are your gods, O Israel, who brought you up out of Egypt.'"

In the ancient world, bulls were a symbol of strength and fertility in an agricultural society, and it was common for people to make a representation of their gods. It only follows, then, that once they got their idol, the Israelites engaged in "revelry," a practice that carries sexual connotations in the Old Testament.

Here's the problem: Israel's desire to worship false gods ran directly counter to God's miraculous and loving work of liberating his people from Egypt. Freedom from Egypt should have meant freedom from idols for Israel. But over and over, Israel kept pining for the good old days in Egypt. Bring on the idols. Bring on the slavery.

Can you imagine such a thing?

Surface and Deep Idols

We like to craft our idols a bit more subtly, but we build them all the same. In our fallen condition, a fundamental tendency resides in worshiping only what we can control. Tim Keller made a distinction between a surface idol and a deep idol. A surface idol creates a means to a deeper idol, which demands ultimate allegiance. A surface idol often appears as a pattern of behavior or an unhealthy concept. A woman always has to have a boyfriend and feels worthless at the thought of being single. An overbearing father puts pressure on his children to perform to earn him respect from neighbors. A businessman works long, unhealthy hours, addicted to the approval of others. A funny person craves the center of attention to feel validated and glorified in the eyes of others. Beneath surface idols reside deep cravings for significance, comfort, security, meaning, approval, and ultimately love.

When we lose sight of the power, grace, and love of God, those deep cravings drive us toward addiction to the idols we desire to control. Keller said, "Jesus must become more beautiful to your imagination, more attractive to your heart, than your idol. If you uproot the idol and fail to 'plant' the love of Christ in its place, the idol will grow back."[1]

To remain free, we must continually examine our lives

and take personal inventory. If Israel had taken an honest account of themselves, they would have understood more clearly their relationship with God and his exclusive claim of the redemptive power on display throughout Exodus. In the awareness of his love and grace, a substitute would never do.

Israel's relationship with God needed repair. Because of the golden-calf episode, God had to withdraw his intimate presence from his people. It would be a violation of God's holiness to remain intimately connected to someone who treats his character as if it were worthless.

God chose Moses to lead Israel for several reasons, not the least of which was his deep desire for the presence of God. For Israel's ongoing temptation to craft idols or return to the captivity of Egypt, Moses offered the antidote: a desire for a loving relationship with God. In his own life, the relationship intensified as Moses desired God's presence and God revealed more and more of himself. God relented to the heart of Moses, revealing himself in mysterious and amazing ways, but none more so than one particular moment recorded in Exodus. "'I will cause all my goodness to pass in front of you, and I will proclaim my name, the LORD, in your presence . . . But,' he said, 'you cannot see my face, for no one may see me and live'" (Exod. 33:19–20).

Moses hid in the cleft of a rock, and he experienced the overwhelming mercy and compassion belonging to even a partial revelation of God's consuming glory. Moses longed for the presence of God in the hearts of his people.

HEALING THE RIFT

In the same way the sin of idolatry breaks Israel's relationship with God, addictions short-wire the intimacy we desire. We long for God's presence in our lives, and the only way to experience that mysterious joy requires a renewal of the broken relationship. Like Moses, our desire shifts toward seeking the presence of God in prayer, meditation, and a growing experience of him.

God desires intimacy with each of us. The real failure of an idol resides in our denial of the character of God. Does he really love me? Will he really take care of me? Can he really be trusted?

Examine the idols of your own making. What in your life is holding you back? What or who are you placing first? A continuing inventory yields an ongoing confession: "God, I've put something ahead of you in my life. I've made it the focus of all my energy and effort. I need you back at the center of my life."

11
Live Out Loud

Months after the accident that left him paralyzed from the neck down, Sherman finds himself face to face with his worst fear—not a continuing physical paralysis, but a spiritual one. He feels he may be losing God. Up through the weekend of the July 4 retreat with his friends, God always seemed to be in the business of protecting him, miraculously rescuing him from years of addiction, sending his mom over just after he had taken bottles of sleeping pills, and giving him the courage to say no to his meth dealer after a seven-year habit. You just can't explain these kinds of things.

In the time of celebration before his accident, Sherman realized the life-giving power of his community of friends, who surrounded and covered and loved him, and what a gift from God they had been. In a life filled with alienation, chaos, and destruction, he saw God restoring his life, day by day and moment by moment, into one of purpose and self-giving.

Once the four-wheeler flipped over, throwing him fifteen feet to the ground, severing his spine between C5 and C6, Sherman began to lose sight of the God he had come to know. It isn't as much an issue of anger as fear. If God cannot be counted on to protect him, who can?

At the depth of his doubt, Mark shows up, as he has frequently, to pray with his best friend for healing. Sherman shares his fear and together, for the first time, they sort through the circumstances following his accident. Miles into the darkening woods with no one around and no cell-phone reception, they heard the voice of a man, who happened to be a paramedic, who managed to call for an ambulance. Five-and-a-half hours later, Sherman underwent an operation under the skill of one of the country's best spinal cord surgeons. When the doctor told Sherman's wife that her husband was leaking spinal cord fluid into his lungs and that he was unstable for another surgery, she asked everyone in the waiting room to pray. Within minutes, his condition stabilized. In an induced coma for forty-five days, Sherman nearly died

*twice, then awoke without a trace of brain damage and was
given a firm prognosis for a life without any movement below
his neck. Following acceptance into a Denver rehabilitation
center ranked third in the nation, Sherman returned home
five months after his injury with feeling in his toes and ankles
and some control of his arms.*

*When Sherman makes a vow to Mark that, with the
continued grace of God, he hopes to walk again, they smile at
each other. At the same time, they recognize together God's
protection and love of Sherman following his accident. As
Mark prays for his friend, Sherman understands the continuing healing as not just physical but also deeply spiritual.*

The Glory of God

Throughout the book of Exodus, God set in motion plans
for the tabernacle, his promise of presence in the midst of
his people. Exodus 40:34 records the consummation of
the work: "The Cloud covered the Tent of Meeting, and
the Glory of God filled The Dwelling" (msg).

Can you imagine the moment? Think of how Steven
Spielberg or James Cameron might imagine it: God in a
hovering cloud by day, fire by night. Radiant and pulsing

with light, casting long shadows into the wilderness, the glory of God animated the tabernacle.

On the outskirts of the Promised Land, Israel was already familiar with God's glory—in a pillar and cloud that protected them from Egypt's armies, in the miracle of the parting of the Red Sea, and in the fire on the distant heights of Mount Sinai. But none of that compares to this. The weight, power, and light of the divine filled the tabernacle.

I love how one commentary describes the divine revelation in the context of God's relationship with his people: "The God of the exodus—the God of power, who made the heavens and the earth; the God of justice, who plagued the Egyptians; the God of love, who kept his covenant with Israel; the God of providence, who led his people through the wilderness; the God of truth, who gave them his law; the God of mercy, who atoned for their sins; the God of holiness, who set them apart for service— this great God was present in glory."[1]

The book of Exodus culminates in the dwelling of God in the tabernacle. From the beginning, as Israel suffered in slavery, God occasionally revealed himself and radically changed the situation. In chapters 25 through 40, God planned for the residency of his glory, the tabernacle, through a series of instructions about blueprints, offerings, ordinances, building materials, and surroundings.

While the glory of God provides reason enough for worship, the amazement of God indwelling his tabernacle deepens in several realities. Consider that the tabernacle:

- Stands in the midst of his people
- Presents an ongoing reality for his people
- Foreshadows an even greater dwelling in the person of Jesus

I love *The Message*'s translation for *tabernacle*: "Dwelling." The tabernacle was not built on a mountain or in a jeweled palace but in the midst of God's people in the wilderness. In residing within the community of Israel, God demonstrated that he has not only come to save his people but ultimately to be in relationship with them. God chose and made his home with Israel out of his love for them. God's glory and power were on display in the world's greatest demonstration of shock and awe, not just for display but to benefit his people.

The verb translated as "fills" in Exodus 40:34 is significant because it reflects an ongoing, dynamic reality. It denotes not a one-time event—that God filled the tabernacle—but that he was continually doing so, each moment renewing his glory. In addition to the present-tense reality of God, the tabernacle was also portable. A large tent, it could be moved from one place to the next. In the context of his ongoing presence and portable dwelling, God was free to lead his people to freedom while remaining in their midst.

The tabernacle foreshadowed an even greater revelation of God's glory for the sake of humankind. In the person of Jesus, "God was pleased to have all his fullness dwell in him" (Col. 1:19), who, in turn, "made his dwelling among us" (John 1:14). *The Message*'s translation of John 1:14 states the reality in contemporary terms:

> The Word became flesh and blood,
>   and moved into the neighborhood.
> We saw the glory with our own eyes,
>   the one-of-a-kind glory,
>   like Father, like Son,

Generous inside and out,
> true from start to finish.

Through God's power and grace, expressed through a loving relationship, we are free.

So now what? Paul wrote, "So Christ has truly set us free. Now make sure that you stay free, and don't get tied up again in slavery" (Gal. 5:1 NLT).

Though Israel often pined for the familiar routines of captivity, and early Christians were tempted to retreat back into the heartless humming of the law, we must desire to stay free in the ongoing grace of Jesus. We must resist the temptations of old habits built on the deceptions of self-fulfillment. If we really believe God dwells with us in power and glory, it frees us to lose the obsession with self and live in love for others.

Jesus stated the paradox of purpose: "For whoever wants to save his life will lose it, but whoever loses his life for me and for the gospel will save it" (Mark 8:35). True life blossoms when we share the love and grace of God with others.

Living Out Loud

In one of my favorite books, *The Ragamuffin Gospel*, Brennan Manning wrote:

> Because salvation is by grace through faith, I believe
> . . . I shall see the prostitute from the Kit-Kat Ranch
> in Carson City, Nevada, who tearfully told me she
> could find no other employment to support her two-
> year-old son. I shall see the woman who had an abor-
> tion and is haunted by guilt and remorse but did the
> best she could faced with grueling alternatives; the
> businessman besieged with debt who sold his integ-
> rity in a series of desperate transactions; the insecure
> clergyman addicted to being liked, who never chal-
> lenged his people from the pulpit and longed for
> unconditional love; the sexually abused teen molested
> by his father and now selling his body on the street,
> who, as he falls asleep each night after his last "trick,"
> whispers the name of the unknown God he learned
> about in Sunday school; the deathbed convert who
> for decades had his cake and ate it, broke every law of
> God and man, wallowed in lust, and raped the earth

. . . If this is not good news to you, you have never understood the gospel of grace.[2]

In the road out of the slavery of our personal captivity, we'll often experience raging waters and deathly odds and violence similar to what the Israelites could see falling in around them. We too will come to know the continuing rescue of a supernatural God working on our behalf and the paradoxes of faith: in powerlessness, transformation; in surrender, a sovereign God; in making amends for torn lives, the wholeness of grace; in unexpected forgiveness, the healing of the soul; and in shattering brokenness, a heart full of Jesus. In the ongoing awareness of a God who leads in a cloud by day and fire by night, the addict feels privileged to choose, with each new day, to serve and live rather than to use and die.

Most of us fool ourselves in our own subtleties. It's easy, we reason, to abuse a little and feel like you are getting away with it. Surf for porn late at night because your wife will never know. Seek the approval of others because we all need encouragement. Obsess about the future because you deserve a better life. Eat ice cream and Snickers because a hard life needs just a little pleasure. Refuse to forgive a friend because he feels no need to change.

We seldom recognize the reality—with each act motivated by lust or anger or greed or self-interest, we sacrifice the full life of living out loud. In his life of dwelling among us, Jesus states his loving intention, "I came so they can have real and eternal life, more and better life than they ever dreamed of" (John 10:10 MSG). Will we take Jesus at his word, or do we through our own efforts continue to carve out another in a string of worthless idols, each failing to fill our lives with purpose, value, joy, and love?

Exodus closes with the ongoing picture: "So the cloud of the LORD was over the tabernacle by day, and fire was in the cloud by night, in the sight of all the house of Israel during all their travels" (Exod. 40:38). We experience the essence of God through faith in his grace.

Imagine the glory of a supernatural God, burning in a cloud by day and a fire by night, leading and transforming you through his power and love. In his grace, you admit your own powerlessness to save yourself and you surrender to the God of the cosmos, who just so happens to be in your corner. Imagine living with the freedom to take a personal inventory of your life—safe in his grace—and seek to make amends to the people you have hurt, extending to others the same kind of grace and love you have experienced. And imagine the community of others finding a mysterious hope, power, and love along the road out to freedom. This is possible, as I and so many others have experienced. Jesus really does set people free, and he desires for you to be free. Reach out to him in faith and trust, and keep walking the path to freedom.

MARKED FOR LIFE

A short time after he walks his first steps with the help of parallel bars, Sherman walks into the tattoo store and explains to the artist what he desires.

As the man begins his work, Sherman barely notices the pain in his enthusiasm to share the reasons for the tattoos he has chosen. As he once again lists the miracles in his life, Sherman realizes it's not so much his story he is sharing, but God's. Sherman's story of addiction would have ended in death or paralysis of soul, but God's story yields redemption, value, and purpose. Sherman's story was about isolation and alienation; God's story casts a community of friends like Mark into the plot. Sherman's story was lost in the dead end of self-seeking; God's story brings new life, an active and animating Spirit precisely at the points of his own helplessness, dependence, surrender, and a desire to make amends and serve others.

When the artist says he is finished, they examine the tattoos together—two words in ink, one on the back of his left arm, the other on the back of his right.

"Truly Blessed" *is what Sherman lives to say.*

Acknowledgments

A special word of thanks to:

The amazing people who allowed their stories to be shared in *Throw It Down*. Even though names and situations were changed to protect anonymity, your courage to share from your life and allow all of us to learn from you is remarkable. Thanks for your transparency and for being willing to go back and reopen some old wounds for the sake of others.

The people and staff of Central Christian Church, who allow me to be myself and who are gracious enough to overlook my faults. I love serving alongside you.

The people of Hillside Christian Church, who loved

me when I was a mess and who were a community for me on the path to freedom.

The *Throw It Down* team: Chris Ferebee, Rob Birkhead, Rob Wilkins, and Bob Wood. You are an amazing group of people to work with. Each of you in your own way made this a much better book.

Lori, the love of my life; the glue that holds our family together; the calming presence no matter how busy life gets.

Emma and Ethan, who bring me so much love and who teach me about God every day. May your lives be characterized by God's freedom.

Jesus, for the best twenty-two years of my life. I am forever grateful.

Notes

Chapter 2: Beautiful Shambles

1. The names and details shared in the stories throughout this book have been changed to protect people's privacy. All stories are used by permission.

Chapter 4: No More Games

1. Eugene Peterson, *Christ Plays in Ten Thousand Places* (Grand Rapids, MI: Eerdmans, 2005), 164–65.

Chapter 5: Grace Spilling Over

1. Henri Nouwen, *Life of the Beloved* (New York: Crossroads, 1992), 21.

Chapter 10: Guard Your Heart

1. Tim Keller, *Counterfeit Gods: The Empty Promises of Money, Sex, and Power, and the Only Hope That Matters* (New York: Dutton, 2009), 172.

Chapter 11: Live Out Loud

1. Philip Graham Ryken, *Exodus: Saved for God's Glory* (Wheaton, IL: Crossway, 2005), 1160.
2. Brennan Manning, *The Ragamuffin Gospel* (Sisters, OR: Multnomah, 2005), 31–32.

About the Author

Jud Wilhite serves as senior pastor of Central Christian Church. More than 17,000 attend Central's campuses each weekend. Jud is the author of several books including *Eyes Wide Open: See and Live the Real You* and *Uncensored Grace: Stories of Hope from the Streets of Vegas.* Jud and his wife, Lori, reside in the Las Vegas area with their two children and a slobbery bulldog named Roxy.

Share Your Thoughts

With the Author: Your comments will be forwarded to the author when you send them to *zauthor@zondervan.com*.

With Zondervan: Submit your review of this book by writing to *zreview@zondervan.com*.

Free Online Resources at
www.zondervan.com

Zondervan AuthorTracker: Be notified whenever your favorite authors publish new books, go on tour, or post an update about what's happening in their lives at www.zondervan.com/authortracker.

Daily Bible Verses and Devotions: Enrich your life with daily Bible verses or devotions that help you start every morning focused on God. Visit www.zondervan.com/newsletters.

Free Email Publications: Sign up for newsletters on Christian living, academic resources, church ministry, fiction, children's resources, and more. Visit www.zondervan.com/newsletters.

Zondervan Bible Search: Find and compare Bible passages in a variety of translations at www.zondervanbiblesearch.com.

Other Benefits: Register yourself to receive online benefits like coupons and special offers, or to participate in research.

ZONDERVAN®

ZONDERVAN.com/
AUTHORTRACKER
follow your favorite authors